Workbook for

The
Editorial Eye

SECOND EDITION

Jane T. Harrigan

Karen Brown Dunlap

Prepared by
George Estrada
Humboldt State University

Bedford/St. Martin's
Boston ◆ New York

For information write: Bedford/St. Martin's, 75 Arlington Street, Boston,
MA 02116   (617-399-4000)

ISBN: 0-312-15756-8

Contents

CHAPTER 1
Editors Today

Exercise I: Editors and Their Tasks

Briefly respond to the following.

1. What do editors do at daily newspapers? Note what your current strengths and weaknesses are.

2. What tasks are you unfamiliar with? Create a plan of how to acquire the knowledge to perform the tasks. For instance, if you are unfamiliar with page layout, what software should you learn? Why?

3. Test the accuracy of your responses to the previous questions. Call or e-mail a copy editor at a daily newspaper, and ask her what she does on a daily, weekly and monthly basis. Ask about her training or the first job she had. Contact editors from both small and large newspapers so that you can compare and contrast their work lives.

Exercise II: Know Your Readers

2-9-06

1. Contact the editors of a local newspaper and ask if they would be willing to share the results of their latest reader demographics research with you. Ask one of the editors how these findings affected their news coverage.

2. What sorts of studies would you conduct to get a clearer picture of what readers in your area want? Explain the reasoning behind your choices.

If there is already a newspaper out, I would put a small questionair or survey in there along with a paid postage envelope for the reader to mail back. It's easy for the reader as well, as the editor.

1

3. How would you go about refining or changing your approach to covering news, knowing what you know about the demographics of your area?

4. A man who claims to be a longtime subscriber calls and complains that your newspaper is covering too many trendy stories, and that you need to stick to "what's really important," like coverage of the city council, planning commission, and community groups. Your latest reader survey strongly contradicts the caller's opinions. What do you do and why?

Think about it, but if he's the only complainer then you need to please everyone else, so I would keep doing what I'm already doing

5. A special-interest group has orchestrated a campaign to get news coverage for an issue. Your newspaper is bombarded with phone calls, faxes and letters, all using similar or identical phrases, from readers threatening to cancel their subscriptions if you do not cover this issue in the way they'd like to have it covered. What do you do and why?

Exercise III: News Judgment

1. How does timeliness affect your judgment of the potential news value of an event? How can timeliness be taken to extremes?

2. How can the prominence of a candidate affect election coverage?

3. What factor in an editor's news judgment might cause an increase in the coverage of community news?

4. When something is a "first" or a "last," it resonates to which component of an editor's news judgment?

5. When a story that is exquisitely written, but otherwise has no real news value, is still placed on the front page, what editorial criteria were used in making that decision?

Maybe there wasn't any hard news that day so the editor decided to introduce a well written story instead.

6. Compare the way four newspapers covered a story. Speculate why each covered it the way it did. Contact an editor at one of the papers and compare his or her reasoning with your own.

7. Give definitions for the following terms:

Localizing

Pack journalism

Packaging

Pass-along readership

Points of entry

Refrigerator journalism

Spin doctor

Exercise IV: Rate the Stories

2-7-06

You are the city editor of a local newspaper. Rate the following stories (1 = highest, 10 = lowest) for their potential usefulness in tomorrow's newspaper. Tell which news judgment criteria went into your decision and discuss why you would or wouldn't run each story. If you decide to run it, discuss how prominently you intend to play it. If you decide not to run the story in tomorrow's paper, explain what you'd do with the information.

_4_ **A:** A city councilman was arrested last week for drunken driving and spent the night in jail.

_2_ **B:** The district attorney's office is still investigating a case involving the serious beating of a prisoner in the county jail last year.

_5_ **C:** A local man who is accused of stalking singer Jennifer Lopez is scheduled to appear in court tomorrow to ask a judge to dismiss the case against him.

_1_ **D:** A local high school teacher who claims he was fired because he is a Muslim hired an attorney today to file a suit against the school district.

_3_ **E:** A local association of Filipino Americans (with membership numbering more than 300). is circulating a petition asking the president of the United States to withdraw military troops from the Philippines. Members say they will send the petition next week.

_10_ **F:** Rock star Trent Reznor was spotted at a local music shop yesterday, checking out synthesizers. A couple of shoppers recognized him and asked for his autograph, but he declined, saying he was in a rush.

_6_ **G:** In a speech before Parliament yesterday, the prime minister of England spoke favorably about an article written a couple of years ago by a political science professor who teaches in a local university.

_2_ **H:** A stockbroker who works for a brokerage firm located in a nearby suburb is indicted today for selling more than $2 million of bogus municipal bonds.

_4_ **I:** A local high school football player is offered a scholarship to Ohio State University, but announces today that he's staying home to work in the family tire business.

_10_ **J:** A local hip-hop artist signs a big recording deal this week with an international label, but a leader of the NAACP publicly denounces him today for his constant use of profanity in his songs.

_2_ **K:** A student journalist at a local community college is found in contempt of court today for not revealing the name of a source, and is put in jail.

_3_ **L:** A local fifth grader today advances to the finals in a national spelling competition.

CHAPTER 2

The Copy Editor's Role

Exercise I: Newsroom Organization

Rank the following jobs in terms of how much you might enjoy them (1 = highest, 10 = lowest), then briefly describe what each does.

Editor in chief

Managing editor

National editor

Foreign editor

Wire editor

News editor

City editor

Entertainment editor

Features editor

Sports editor

Business editor

Photo editor

Political editor

Chief copy editor

Copy editor

Copy clerk

Exercise II: Copy Flow

Briefly describe how each of these stories might flow through a newsroom's editing hierarchy (example: from assistant city editor, to city editor, to copy desk, to assistant managing editor, to managing editor).

1. A local man is arrested for a two-year series of armed robberies.

2. A local woman wins the state lottery and donates all the money to charity.

3. A successful community college basketball coach is hired as an assistant coach by the University of Southern California.

4. A state senator representing a local district announces his candidacy for governor.

5. Bruce Springsteen announces that he will do a benefit concert in your area to help the homeless.

6. A kindergarten student finds an old coin in an abandoned school basement. It turns out to be a rare 1804 Bust dollar, which could be worth millions at auction.

7. Singer Shania Twain visits a local school to give an inspirational talk about music, dancing and staying in school.

8. The New York Times wire service reports that a man from your local area has been arrested by FBI agents in Washington, D.C., on suspicion of being involved with the September 11, 2001, attacks on the World Trade Center in New York.

9. The president of Mexico announces he will be visiting your state and your city next month to speak on immigration issues.

10. A local teen wins a national investing contest, having turned a hypothetical $50,000 portfolio of stocks and bonds into $560,000 in three months of trading.

Exercise III: Working with Writers

CASE STUDY #1

You are the editor of your college newspaper. You send one of your reporters to cover a guest lecture on campus by the editor of a Northern California-based daily newspaper. Your reporter attends the lecture, takes notes and makes a few phone calls, but becomes ill before he can write the story. Your deadline is in three hours. You hurriedly pick an available staff writer to construct a story from the sick reporter's notes. Here is what you have.

1. Connie Rux, editor of the Eureka Times-Standard, said she knew she wanted to be a journalist since the eighth grade.

2. Rux visited a beginning reporting class on your campus yesterday and spoke about her experiences in journalism.

3. Rux has been editor for more than three years at the Times-Standard. Before going to Eureka, she was a section editor at the Oakland Tribune. The Eureka area ranks 189th in media market size in the United States. The Oakland-San Francisco area ranks fifth. Eureka is located in Humboldt County, the Redwood Coast area of California, about 280 miles north of San Francisco.

4. In a phone interview, Mac McClary, a professor of journalism at Humboldt State University, had good things to say about Rux. In addition to making the paper more attractive, Rux has also utilized "creative use of color" and "has been able to work with limited resources," McClary said.

5. Rux is the first woman to be appointed editor of the Times-Standard in the paper's 125-year history.

6. Rux said, "It is very important for up-and-coming journalists to have a positive role model who has strived and succeeded in the marketplace."

7. A native of Fort Worth, Rux began her career at small newspapers in Texas. She said she initially was "given soft assignments and was not given the chance to prove myself on the front line."

8. When she first moved to California, she got a job at the Orange County Register.

9. Ben Hoffman, who is the Times-Standard's entertainment editor, said he enjoys working with Rux and describes her as "laid-back" and "very forgiving." Hoffman is a graduate of Humboldt State University.

10. Rux's husband, Jack Rux, also joined the Times-Standard as sports editor. He also has a long, distinguished career in journalism. As a sports reporter for the Oakland Tribune, he covered the San Francisco 49ers during the Joe Montana era.

11. In response to a student question about missing the Bay Area, Rux said, "I love this area because it is peaceful and beautiful. I miss the excitement of the big city, but there's nothing like this area for overall quality of life."

Write short answers for these questions.

1. How do you advise your second reporter on the writing of this story?

2. Do you have enough for a story, or do you need more information?

3. What do you think is the lead?

4. Is there anything in this story that needs developing?

5. Is there enough quote material, or do you need more?

6. Is there enough context, or do you need more?

7. How would you award bylines? Would you give it just to the first reporter, just the second, or would you give a double byline?

Exercise IV: Professional Qualities of Copy Editors

1. What traits and talents must a good editor have?

2. Do you have the talent and temperament to be a good editor? Why or why not?

3. Imagine you are applying for a copy-editing job at the local newspaper. What traits would you emphasize on your résumé? Make up a résumé that highlights those traits.

CHAPTER 3
Editing for Grammar

Exercise I: Nouns, Plurals and Possessives

Edit the following sentences using the proper copy-editing symbols. Also, change inappropriate words.

1. The professor said the grades on the first paper's were mostly Bs.

2. He had a collection of comics from the 1960s and 70s that were quite valuable.

3. Jackie Chans' movies tend to have a lot of action.

4. The Oakland A's named their new manager yesterday.

5. Smith and Robertson's abandoned motorcycles were found on an isolated road.

6. The class's dilemma was that the teacher was a very tough grader.

7. In the end, the win was the Republicans', not the Democrats.

8. It is not an issue of ethics', but of simple common sense.

9. The baseball commissioner's decision to cancel the opening day games led to fans protesting outside stadiums in several cities yesterday.

10. The university president expressed equal displeasure with his team and the opposition's behavior after the game.

Exercise II: Pronouns

Choose the appropriate pronoun in the following sentences, making sure it matches the key noun.

1. The Golden State Warriors will hold (its, their) annual benefit luncheon today.

2. The Lakers coaching staff will plot (its, their) strategy for the fourth quarter.

3. The Supreme Court will announce (its, their) decision tomorrow.

4. The softball team from Montana (is, are) traveling to New Jersey for the tournament.

5. The group of Japanese tourists reviewed (its, their) itinerary at the airport coffee shop.

6. The class (is, are) debating the merits of learning manual headline counting.

7. More than one-third of the student body (is, are) nationally recognized scholars.

8. This particular squad of soldiers (answers, answer) directly to the captain.

9. The East Coast panel of newspaper editors said (it is, they are) looking for talented interns who can work well on deadline.

10. None of the stamps in his collection (is, are) from Nicaragua.

11. Every journalist at that student newspaper has (his or her, their) stories checked for AP style.

12. The prosecutor argued that the defendants' motive was (his, their) greed.

13. The League of Women Voters (has, have) expressed (its, their) position on that issue.

14. The United Latinos of Alameda County (has, have) made (its, their) position clear.

15. The team (is, are) arguing about the merit system installed by the new coach.

Exercise III: Verbs

Indicate the tense and mood of the verbs (infinitive, present, past, future, past perfect, present perfect, future perfect tense; indicative, imperative, conditional, subjunctive mood).

1. I will have completed the project by noon tomorrow.

2. She could be finished sooner if she weren't such a perfectionist.

3. The guitarist from Spain had played what the audience came to hear.

4. Is it possible that the senator miscalculated the mood of his constituents?

5. The chief of police hears from the mayor every day.

6. The investor has picked Nokia as the most undervalued stock.

7. Will the tourists from Taiwan arrive in time for the World Series?

8. The dancer could leap higher if she wanted to.

9. She would do well if she studied the right things.

10. The young singer pranced about as if she were Madonna.

11. It is important that reporters be committed to their deadlines.

12. The student council member had acted as if he were president of the student body.

Exercise IV: Similar Words

Pick the right word in the following sentences.

1. The prosecutor (laid, lay) the evidence on the table and addressed the jury.

2. The remains of the Titanic have (lay, laid, lain) on the floor of the Atlantic for close to 90 years.

3. The baby was seen (lying, laying, laid) peacefully in his crib.

4. The professor (lay, layed, laid) the blame on the student's laziness.

5. He (lay, laid, lied) down for just a few minutes.

6. The general manager's daughter (sung, has sung) the national anthem several times at the team's home games.

7. The English professor (teached, taught, has taught) that subject many times before.

8. The student from El Salvador (went, has gone) to California in 1999.

9. Before she realized it, she (drank, drunk, had drank, had drunk) four beers.

10. He (swum, has swam, has swum) the waters off the northern coast of Maui.

Exercise V: Tense

Give the past tense and past perfect tense of the following irregular verbs. (Use first person form.)

1. to eat (Example: I eat, I ate, I had eaten.)

2. to broadcast

3. to drink

4. to cling

5. to weave

6. to hang

7. to strike

8. to bear

9. to do

10. to sing

11. to catch

12. to bring

13. to tear

14. to swim

15. to drink

16. to become

17. to stand

18. to go

19. to shine

20. to light

Exercise VI: Spelling

Correct the following misspelled words.

abstaine	calibre
abundent	catsup
abysmel	caveot
accomodation	chaufeur
accountible	collegue
accreu	commitee
acoutrement	concommitant
acquital	consortiom
affidavid	coockoo
affinnity	coup detat
ajunct	cymbiotic
apocalyps	defendent
aquaintance	demagog
cacophoney	diservice

donut

enquire

equalled

equitible

esthetic

exagerrate

expresso

filibustre

fullfil

fundamentle

galaxie

gormet

habeus corpus

halleluyah

headach

hearsaye

hemorrage

hypothettical

imposter

innocuose

inpenetrable

insurection

inuendo

judgement

legalease

liveable

luminesense

lustruos

Massachusettes

miniscule

naeve

numismatix

ordenance

pendalum

plyers

profaine

prosecuter

purile

rebutal

reconnasance

rehtoric

reknowned

reminise

remitt

renassance

resiliant

resistence

resonansce

resplendant

rhythym

sacreligious

sanatarium

secretery	subteranean
sedement	succesion
seperate	sucsinct
shiney	supercede
shrapnell	symbal
smoulder	synagog
sollemn	towards
solliloquy	travelog
specemin	tsar
statuetory	vehiment
stedfast	virtuose

Exercise VII: Jargon

It is often better to use simpler language, especially when writing hard news for a daily newspaper. Find simpler words for the following.

1. writing utensil	12. conversant
2. disingenuous	13. infinitesimal
3. egalitarian	14. pro forma
4. equivocation	15. paean
5. milieu	16. eschew
6. putative	17. patrician
7. ontology	18. reciprocate
8. disequilibrium	19. capitulate
9. foment	20. typology
10. incapacitated	21. ruminate
11. convalescence	22. languid

23. plenary

24. plebiscite

25. parsimonious

26. subjugate

27. rubric

28. erudite

29. multiperspectival

30. modernity

Exercise VIII: Similar Words

Circle the correct word in the following sentences.

1. His friends tried to (convince, persuade) him to attend Oregon State University.

2. Stalin's body (lied, laid, lay) in state at the Kremlin.

3. He decided to major in forestry because he loved the natural (ecology, environment).

4. (Over, more than) 20,000 fans attended the concert that weekend.

5. The (further, farther) he went, the closer he got to his goal.

6. In his closing statement, the defendant's lawyer attempted to (rebut, rebuke, refute) the expert's testimony.

7. The president did not make his position clear, so White House reporters were forced to (infer, deduce) what he meant.

8. The prisoner (flaunts, flouts) the law.

9. She had (less, fewer) admirers than her sister had.

10. The contract has run (its, it's) course, so now (its, it's) up to the arbitrators to decide the issue.

11. The three friends looked at (each other, one another) and knew what the answer would have to be.

12. There were tacklers on (each, either) side of the Northwestern running back as he approached the Iowa goal line.

13. He (pled, pleaded) (innocent, not guilty) to the manslaughter charges.

14. The (murdered, slain) man's family attended the trial of the suspected (killer, murderer).

15. The attorney (counciled, counseled) his client on the procedures for preliminary hearings.

16. The brash young student was not very (discreet, discrete) with his opinions.

17. She was charged with (drunk, drunken) driving and spent the night in (jail, prison).

18. He (pored, poured) over the AP style manual the night before the midterm exam.

19. The kindergarten (pupils, students) at Fruitvale Elementary School were visited by Barney the dinosaur yesterday.

20. Tennis great Jimmy Connors helped to usher in the age of the metal tennis (racket, racquet).

21. The sophomore contrasted his economics professor (with, to) his journalism and English professors. He said the economics professor was much different (than, from) the others in classroom demeanor.

22. The rock critic was used to receiving (complimentary, complementary) tickets to local concerts.

23. Libelous statements do harm to one's (character, reputation).

24. The student council voted to (censor, censure, sensor) the vice president's actions.

25. His collection is (composed, comprised) of silver dollars from the defunct Carson City mint.

Exercise IX: Capitalization and Trademark Names

Capitalize appropriately those words that are proper trademark names. If the word is a common noun, leave it lowercased. (See AP style manual and other sources.)

aspirin   cognac

band-aid   cola

beer   cottage cheese

bourbon   dacron

boy scouts   dixie cup

brandy   dumpster

fax	q-tips
fiberglas	refrigerator
frigidaire	scotch whiskey
frisbee	styrofoam
graham crackers	technicolor
hamburgers	teflon
howitzer	teleprompter
iodine	telescope
jeep	thermos
jell-o	touch-tone
jukebox	trampoline
kerosene	tylenol
kleenex	uzi
linotype	valium
magnum	velcro
microwave	volleyball
mimeograph	windbreaker
panorama	xerox
plexiglas	yo-yo
porsche	

Exercise X: More Capitalization and Trademark Names

Edit the following sentences. Replace trademark words with common words, unless it occurs inside a quote. If using a brand name is absolutely necessary, capitalize it appropriately. (Note: Not all sentences have a trademark noun.)

1. The office manager told him to xerox a large stack of papers.

2. "I want you to xerox those papers," the manager told the clerk.

3. He searched through the dumpster for food.

4. He attached his picks to his guitar with velcro strips.

5. She heated her dinner in her new microwave oven.

6. She ordered a glass of burgundy wine, but he ordered a budweiser.

7. He put some dixie cups in the bathroom for his guests.

8. He acquired a love of jeeps while serving in the Army.

9. She saw it was a bit cold outside, so she put on a sweater and a windbreaker.

10. He said he felt "like a yo-yo" as he bounced on the trampoline.

11. He put some band-aids on his cuts and poured a cup of coffee from his thermos.

12. She felt a sneeze coming on, so she pulled a kleenex from her pocket.

13. She was on a diet, so she ordered jell-o, cottage cheese, graham crackers and sourdough bread for lunch.

14. He cut class to watch the frisbee tournament.

15. Police found a .44-caliber magnum in the suspect's car.

16. He referred to the muzak playing in the background as "elevator music."

17. The patient asked for nitrous oxide, but the dentist said that novocain was all that was needed.

Exercise XI: Spelling

Correct the misspellings of common words and proper names in the following sentences. Also make sure nouns are correctly capitalized. Use a dictionary and the AP style manual for common words. Use reference sources (traditional and online) to check proper names.

1. Soviet premiere Nikita Khruschev pounded his shoe on a table at the United Nations in 1960 to protest a speech by a British politician.

2. The law student from Mississipi played CDs by Snoop Doggy Dog and Doctor Dre to make his point about freedom of speech.

3. The legal council for the defendents prepared to make his presentation to the jury.

4. She drank a Doctor Pepper because she figured she needed a dose of caffein to keep awake for another two hours.

5. Palestinian leader Yasser Arafat met with President Jimmy Carter on that fateful day in 1979.

6. "I will have to use my best judgement," the congressman from Missourri said in reponse to a question about a possible run for the Presidency.

7. The economics student from Nigeria received mostly A's and B's during his freshmen year at Georgetown.

8. The blues fan from Japan collected recordings of his favorite American musicians, including Buddy Guy, Robert Cray and Stevie Ray Vaughn.

9. The business student from Peru decided to run for vice-president of the student body.

10. The dissident author was jailed by Italian facists during the years immediately preceeding World War 2.

11. The new disk jockey at the student radio station decided to play more rock and roll during the late evening.

12. "I am proud to be a member of the priviledged class," the student from Oxford said. "There is no nobility in poverty."

13. Many in the crowd expected the Holocaust revisionist to wear a Swastika on his sleeve.

14. He practiced Buddism for many years, but he said he became a Moslem after his visit to Morroco two years ago.

15. Her new zip-code in Alameda, Calif., was 94501.

16. She elected to take classes in Native American film to fulfil some of her general education requirments in the humanities.

Exercise XII: Compound Modifiers and Hyphens

Find the compound modifiers in the following sentences and hyphenate them appropriately. (Note: Not all sentences have a compound modifier.)

1. He had a number of rare date coins in his dime collection.

2. The city council had a heated debate about the military parade issue.

3. The computer lab had an assortment of low and high resolution monitors.

4. Many in the know investors are buying high tech stocks while prices are depressed, the analyst said.

5. The 19 year old right handed pitcher had a Roger Clemens like fastball.

6. He had a 3 inch cut on his forehead after falling off the 6 foot high platform.

7. He was a classically trained violinist, but he had a punk rock attitude.

8. Police found a 3 pound bag of high grade marijuana in the suspect's car.

9. This Sunday will be a sports lover's dream.

10. He was one of those prototypical old school coaches, the young athlete reckoned.

11. The seriocomic, anti intellectual play earned praise from the New York Times critic.

12. It was an already done deal, but the prosecution produced a last minute demand for a lengthier probationary period.

13. The commander in chief had a difficult decision to make.

14. The middle school students from Phoenix have a chance to visit Hollywood this year.

15. Her horse won first and second place awards at the regional show in Dallas.

Exercise XIII: Improper Use of Modifiers

Edit the following sentences for improper use of modifying terms.

1. She found that she was quite pregnant.

2. Her work was totally perfect.

3. The stamp from Uruguay was the most unique one in his collection.

4. The victim was already dead when police arrived.

5. He had hardly anything to buy food with except for a few pennies and nickels.

Exercise XIV: Periods, Commas, Colons and Semicolons

Punctuate the following sentences properly.

1. The senator visited four states during his western campaign swing; Washington, Oregon, Nevada, and Utah.

2. Arson investigators found traces of gasoline inside the living room area and they began searching for more clues.

3. Boston Red Sox fans bemoan the so-called "Curse of the Bambino," and anticipate failure with each season.

4. The play "Evita" was turned into a film, starring Madonna.

5. The Beatles' first movie, "A Hard Day's Night," was a masterpiece of filmmaking by director, Richard Lester.

6. When Anna Kournikova stepped into the room all the sportswriters turned their heads.

7. Drama teacher, Richard Jones, chose "The Wizard of Oz," for this semester's student production.

8. Joe Williams was cast as the Tin Man, Paris Doss was picked to play the Scarecrow, the Lion was rendered royally by Martin Kingsbury, and George Estrada played the ubiquitous Wizard.

9. At the buffet-style restaurant he sampled pork chop suey, tomato beef chow yuke, beef with oyster sauce and duck.

10. The fans hoped for a dramatic, intense, competitive, game.

11. His mission was explained clearly to him, the young fighter pilot knew what he had to do.

12. The job candidate met with Frank Finney, the executive editor and Cheryl Lee, the personnel director.

13. The American tourists told their Danish friend, that they found Copenhagen fascinating.

14. The journalism student thought that his story was perfect but he neglected to check for AP style errors.

15. He had a mint-condition copy of the first Spider-Man comic, he knew he could get a lot of money for it.

Exercise XV: Quotation Marks

Edit the following for proper use of quotation marks and punctuation. Also, if necessary, fix sentences that don't quite work.

1. "We are quite proud of our football team", the president of Ohio State University said. "They've brought a national championship to Columbus".

2. The All-American volleyball player decided to go to Texas A&M University because she's, "an Aggie to my soul."

3. Jefferson's sister asked him "What in heaven's name were you thinking"?

4. "The Russians have a tough squad," James Smith, the coach of the U.S. team said. We are facing our biggest challenge of the Olympics."

5. Marty Gonzalez, an anchorman for a San Francisco television station, said "Journalism is the most interesting profession in the world."

6. The English professor from Penn State addressed the conference and said "The post-modern age is upon us. Definitions are changing, borders are shifting, and everything we know is wrong."

7. She said, she went to Idaho during Christmas break to stay with family, visit friends and, "just go bumming around my old neighborhood."

8. The young scholar from England often used Shakespeare's famous line about the slings and arrows of outrageous fortune.

9. Her grandmother's favorite songs are Heartbreak Hotel by Elvis Presley and Maybelline by Chuck Berry.

10. "Did you know?" he asked his friend from Arkansas, "That we do things a lot different here in New York?" The friend just shrugged and said, he didn't care.

11. "I find it very hard to believe that this fountainhead of capitalism," the American tourist said after arriving in Hong Kong, "is part of communist China."

12. Her friend from Mexico told her "Vaya con dios," which means, God be with you. She replied, "What"?

13. "By any means necessary," was perhaps the most memorable of the sayings of slain activist Malcolm X.

14. "I'm not really sure how I got the nickname," the former football star said. "Just one day teammates started saying, hey Big Dog, hey Big Dog. And it just stuck."

15. He checked out three books from the library: a book on Cuban history, a "travel guide" to Spain, and the Ernest Hemingway novel, The Sun Also Rises.

16. How many people attended the opening-day screening of "The Lord of the Rings?" Estimates varied, but attendance records were broken in many big cities.

17. Her acting résumé includes appearances on Baywatch, Touched by an Angel, the Spider-Man movie and a "Spring Break" special on MTV.

18. "The phrases I do, I promise and I swear are not synonymous," the linguist explained.

19. She said that she owns every recording Bob Marley ever made, and that the album Natty Dread is her "all-time, all-world, favorite".

20. "I don't care how many times you tell me 'you're an idiot for loving that guy," she told her mother, "I will never stop loving him."

Exercise XVI: Noun-Verb Agreement

Pick the verb that best fits these sentences.

1. His cousin, regarded by many as the smartest and most accomplished member of the family, (is, are) a Wall Street lawyer.

2. His mother and sisters (is, are) cooking dinner tonight.

3. His brothers or his father (is, are) picking up his sister from work.

4. Either his friend or his cousin (is, are) going to the game with him.

5. Neither his CDs nor his Rolex watch (was, were) missing.

6. A pessimist and an optimist (do not, does not) often get along.

7. The Brazilian musical group, as well as the salsa orchestra from Cuba, (is, are) joining the tour tomorrow.

8. Each couple and all single travelers (is, are) required to book a room for at least three nights.

9. Neither the tourists from Latvia nor their American hosts (is, are) aware of the situation.

10. Neither the tourists from Sweden nor the American travel agency (is, are) aware of the situation.

11. "Romeo and Juliet" (is, are) his favorite play.

12. Bacon and eggs (is, are) her favorite breakfast.

Exercise XVII: Adjectives and Adverbs

Pick the adjective or adverb that best fits these sentences.

1. She finished her test (quicker, more quickly) than the other students.

2. The golfer from Sacramento felt (bad, badly) about beating his opponent so (thorough, thoroughly).

3. The wine from France was (more tasty, tastier) than the one from Germany.

4. Her attitude was (sassier, more sassy) after returning from college.

5. The freshman quarterback played (good, well) in the big game.

6. He rode his skateboard (real, really) fast while listening to his Metallica tapes.

7. He looked (confident, confidently) as he approached the podium.

8. He danced (jerky, jerkily) to the strange music.

9. She looked (fearful, fearfully) at the new roller coaster.

10. The World Series losers were not (gracious, graciously) in defeat.

11. He appeared (angry, angrily) when he spoke at the public hearing.

12. The prison guard tried her best to treat inmates (impartial, impartially).

Exercise XVIII: Conjunctions

Respond briefly to the following.

1. What do conjunctions do?

2. How are coordinating and correlative conjunctions similar and how are they different?

3. Is it acceptable practice to start a sentence with "and" or "but"?

4. What is the principle of "equal ideas, equal weight"?

5. When you read two ideas connected by "and," what must be checked?

6. Can a subordinate clause contain a main idea?

7. What can be done with a sentence containing too many subordinated ideas?

Exercise XIX: Conjunctions and Weights

Edit these sentences to assign more weight to the greater concept.

1. The fellowships carry a tuition waiver and the opportunity to earn a doctorate.

2. Induction into the Hall of Fame brings with it a gold-plated plaque and a permanent place in baseball history.

3. The brain surgeon said that his research has helped save many lives and brought widespread recognition to his hospital.

4. The reporter from The Chicago Tribune said that her work gives her the feeling that she is somehow making a difference and earning a "pretty decent" salary.

5. The television crew went to Chile to do a travel segment and to film an interview with the new president.

6. The producer went to Hollywood to pitch a movie deal and to watch a Lakers game.

7. The cartoon series creator said she wanted to help children learn basic social skills and find a way to keep her own 3-year-old son entertained.

8. The anthropologist said that the funeral practices of east Ghana were visually stunning and a great way for families there to honor their relatives.

9. The chimp came to the zoo 40 years ago and is the oldest living male chimp in the world.

10. The women's basketball team was nationally ranked for most of the season and lost the first game of the playoff semifinal round.

Exercise XX: Prepositions

Respond briefly to the following.

1. A preposition establishes a relationship between what kinds of words?

2. Is it all right to end a sentence with a preposition?

3. What is the difference between "like" and "as"?

Exercise XXI: Misplaced Prepositional Phrases

Edit the following.

1. The Oakland police sergeant was found guilty of extortion by an Alameda County judge.

2. The New York Yankees shortstop was charged with an error by the official scorer.

3. When she arrived on campus yesterday, the history scholar from the Philippines was given a book by Thomas Jefferson.

4. The main character of the movie "Daredevil" was criticized as being "too disturbed" by the film critic.

5. American troops encountered little resistance by the southern border of the city.

Exercise XXII: Sentence Structure/Modifiers

Edit the following.

1. Researching a book on China, satellite dishes in the provinces seemed out of place.

2. Covering an athletic event, statistics and game highlights are important.

3. Determining the value of old coins, luster, degree of preservation and rarity come into play.

4. Watching the "Woodstock" movie, Carlos Santana, Jimi Hendrix and the Who impressed her the most.

5. With an effective job search, it's good to have an updated résumé, a list of appropriate references and a great cover letter.

Exercise XXIII: Sentence Structure/Parallelism

Edit the following.

1. The fans came to see this historic reunion concert, to hear the band's new songs and the new stadium was also an attraction.

2. The university president said that academic departments could face cuts in operating budgets, decreases in new faculty searches and class offerings might be limited to only core curriculum courses.

3. The well-heeled collector loved to acquire mint-condition specimens of Michael Jordan rookie cards, Willie Mays cards from the 1950s and football legend Bart Starr was also one of his favorites, especially cards from the Green Bay Packers' championship years.

4. The exchange student from Japan complained of how the movie "Pearl Harbor" depicted the Japanese as being ruthless, brutal and made to look "plain," and how the Americans in contrast looked "very glamorous."

5. She needed a new guitar, but she couldn't decide whether she wanted an electric, an acoustic or if she really wanted a new banjo instead.

6. The ambitious young singer bought a karaoke machine, a wireless microphone, a collection of Celine Dion CDs and signed up for lessons.

7. The Pentagon spokesman said that U.S. troops had either entered the target area by parachute drop or in the motorized vehicles that arrived later.

8. Like the FBI, the extensive use of undercover agents is a common practice in big-city police departments.

9. The Washington Post editor said he is looking for interns who are skilled in grammar, spelling, punctuation and have a broad knowledge of world affairs.

10. The anchorman practiced his pronunciation, delivery and how well he could time the reading of his scripts.

11. She found cleaning the refrigerator herself easier than to argue with her husband about doing it.

12. Much of the early work of the Beatles was inspired and gave tribute to Elvis Presley, Chuck Berry and Buddy Holly.

CHAPTER 4
Editing for Style

Exercise I: AP Style: Job Titles

Edit the following sentences, using the AP style manual rules for capitalization of proper job titles and lowercase style for occupational descriptions.

1. Joseph Estrada, the former President of the Philippines, was jailed on corruption charges.

2. Barbara Boxer, a U.S. Senator from California, once served as a Congresswoman from Marin County.

3. Robert Kennedy served as Attorney General during the administration of Pres. John Kennedy, his brother.

4. The humanitarian award was given to former president Jimmy Carter during ceremonies at the White House yesterday.

5. Jason Giambi, the First Baseman of the New York Yankees, added another dangerous left-handed bat to the lineup.

6. Led Zeppelin's lead singer Robert Plant was the prototypical hard-rock frontman, said Charles Young, a Rock Critic from Rolling Stone magazine.

7. According to Sergeant Don Demain, the suspect was once the Principal of a local high school.

8. Arson inspectors will be brought to the scene, said Captain Jay Quiros.

9. United Nations secretary general Kofi Anan had an informal meeting yesterday with the delegates from the African nations.

10. The Chinese Students Association chairwoman, Xiaoni Chen, spoke at length with the new President of the University of Texas.

Exercise II: AP Style: Cities and States

Edit the following sentences, using the AP style manual rules for use of cities, states and abbreviations.

1. This year's debate competition, which was held in Honolulu, Hawaii, attracted teams from as far away as Bangor, Maine, and Miami, Florida.

2. The band from Athens, Georgia, reached its pinnacle with a New Year's Eve concert at the London Palladium.

3. She wants to attend Yale University, but New Haven, Conn. is a long way from her hometown of Paris, TX.

4. The leaders of the Black Student Caucus were from colleges in Calif., N.Y. and Penn.

5. The governor left his mansion in Austin yesterday for a South American tour that would bring him to Lima, Rio de Janeiro and Buenos Aires.

6. The top draft choice of the Carolina Panthers attended Stanford University in Palo Alto, California.

7. The bombings in Oklahoma City, Okla., dominated the front pages of newspapers around the country the next morning.

8. He sent Christmas cards to friends in Indianapolis, Milwaukee and Charlotte last year.

9. The flamenco group from Madrid, Spain, performed in Columbus, Ohio, Minneapolis, Minn., Fargo, N.D, and Juneau, Alaska.

10. The ensemble from Hamburg played selections from Mozart during its tour of universities in the New England states.

Exercise III: AP Style: Numbers

Edit the following sentences, using the AP style manual rules for use of numerals.

1. The Bull Moose Party candidate for student body president won by a margin of 720 votes, outpolling his closest rival by a 2 to 1 ratio.

2. The House subcommittee approved the bill by a vote of nine to seven.

3. The 16 year old student from Detroit beat 9 of the top students from across the nation in the mathematics competition.

4. The boy was three years old when he went to live with his grandparents in Boston.

5. He counted three nickels, two dimes and eleven pennies in his pocket.

6. The number one player in the tournament showed her competitive fire by putting brilliantly on the 2nd and 3rd holes of the playoff round.

7. She drove south on U.S. highway five on her way to Los Angeles.

8. "The 1980's were a memorable decade," the singer from the Flock of Seagulls said.

9. The professor instructed him to turn to page 44 of his case law book.

10. The single mother from Davenport, Iowa, won $55,000,000 in the state lottery.

11. The World War 2 veteran had a collection of ten vintage shotguns and two machine guns.

12. Police officers in Baton Rouge received a pay increase of five percent, but their colleagues from New Orleans got four percent.

13. The Oakland A's finished in 1st place in the American League West last year, but the 2nd-place Anaheim Angels won the World Series.

14. The student leader from Baltimore claimed the first amendment right to say whatever she wanted at the public forum.

15. He inherited about a half-million dollars when his uncle died.

16. The rock 'n' roll festival in Seattle featured the B-52's and Nine Inch Nails.

17. The American Revolution was successful partly because of the ineptitude and failing health of King George the second of England.

18. The journalist from northern California was born on February 1st, 1953.

19. The criminologist from New Jersey said that according to past studies, such unusual crimes occur only once every 25.5 years.

20. Last semester more than 1100 students transferred to the university.

Exercise IV: Redundancy

Eliminate the redundancies in the following.

1. He tried to do some last-minute shopping on Christmas Day, but most of the stores were closed.

2. The family attended Mass together on Easter Sunday.

3. Most of the coins in his coin collection are silver dime 10-cent pieces.

4. He voted against the proposed ordinance even though he knew the consensus of opinion favored it.

5. He said that his benefactor was very kind to him, and that he was "quite magnanimous, actually."

6. A number of famous celebrities endorsed the senatorial candidate.

7. Arson investigators were called to the scene to see if the fire had been set on purpose.

8. The murder suspect was charged with allegedly slaying three people in a killing spree last summer.

9. Two pounds of hashish, three ounces of cocaine and two ounces of narcotics were allegedly found in the suspect's car, police said.

10. A sawed-off shotgun, an Uzi and three automatic weapons were found in the suspect's closet, police said.

11. In attendance at the Jackie Robinson tribute were Yogi Berra, Willie Mays, Sandy Koufax and former players for the Brooklyn Dodgers and Los Angeles Dodgers.

12. The rhythm and blues festival drew big crowds at its shows in England, Sweden, Denmark, Holland, Germany and the Netherlands.

13. The exchange students from Asia seemed to get along well with the exchange students from Australia and India.

14. The high-tech recruiter told the engineering students there would be many job opportunities in the weeks, months and years ahead.

15. The British band is from Liverpool, England, the hometown of the Beatles.

16. The Detroit Red Wings are returning home to the Motor City after this week-long road trip.

17. The student body president knew he had the unanimous support of the entire student council.

18. The incumbent senator launched a campaign swing through four Eastern states.

19. Acta, the first daily newspaper, was created by decree of Roman emperor Julius Caesar to provide the citizens of Rome with daily reports of senate proceedings.

Exercise V: Using Quotes/Eliminating Redundancy

Rewrite these passages to eliminate redundancy or to provide proper setups.

1. The English major won this year's student of the year award. "It was great winning the student of the year award," he said. "It is the biggest thrill of my life."

2. The quarterback said that the team would have to work well together to pull off an upset this weekend. "It will take a total team effort," he said. "But if we play up to our potential, we can win the game."

3. The attorney general is scheduled to give the commencement address next month. "We are very excited to have him here," said university president Martha McKinney. "The commencement ceremonies will certainly benefit from the presence of the attorney general."

4. A high-grade collection of silver dollars will be auctioned by the Future Economists Society to raise money for club activities. "Last year's end-of-term party was great," said club president Mike Lyons. "It was the best party on campus."

5. Rapper Chuck D. from the notorious group Public Enemy said he is looking forward to the concert in Columbus, Ohio. "Our new CD breaks new ground," he said in an interview yesterday. "Our fans will have to open their minds a little bit."

6. The U.S. Olympic basketball team features four players 7 feet tall or more. "Our team feels good about our chances this year," said the head coach. "Make no mistake about it, the road to the gold medal passes through the United States."

7. The figure skating champion from Finland became a U.S. citizen last year. "I've been bad. I haven't practiced in two months," she said. "But I hope to get back in shape by next year's trials."

8. The young businessman from Mexico made his fortune starting a discount moving business in East Los Angeles. "I love going to baseball games," he said. "I reserve weekends for baseball."

9. The former senator is now working as a legislative consultant for several high-tech firms. "My family and I love visiting Washington," she said. "We lived there for 12 years and still have lots of friends in the area."

10. When he saw the academic challenges ahead of him, the young Stanford professor realized he'd have his hands full. "My friends from Berkeley are going to razz me for joining the Stanford faculty," he said. "Berkeley-Stanford is such a big rivalry. I'm going to have fun at the Big Game this year."

Exercise VI: Setting Up Quotes

Edit these passages to eliminate redundancy, set up quotes properly and use attribution more effectively.

1. "I can really relate to Spider-Man because of his complicated personal life, because his problems are so similar to the problems most young adults have," the young comics fan said, explaining why Spider-Man is his favorite superhero.

2. "I got this one when I met my ex-girlfriend last year, then I got this broken heart one when we split up, then I got this new one on my chest when I met my current girlfriend last month," said the singer, explaining the reasons for his tattoos.

3. "I cannot believe she did that after all we've done for her, after all those years of training and after all those years with her teammates," said the volleyball coach, expressing surprise about the sudden resignation of the team captain.

4. "It was great returning to my homeland and seeing how the people live, and experiencing the culture intimately for the first time in my life," said the young entrepreneur, whose parents immigrated to America from Thailand, about her recent trip to Bangkok.

5. "I don't care if it's freezing cold. It just feels great to sit in the Dog Pound and root for the team and be with all my friends from high school," said the young football fan about the invigorating experience of sitting in the end zone at Cleveland Browns games and getting rowdy with his buddies.

6. "I cannot believe I found this in my grandfather's collection, and I cannot believe he just gave it to me without even considering how much it's worth," the 14-year-old said of the mint-condition Mickey Mantle rookie card his grandfather gave to him, a card that experts estimate could be worth up to $100,000 at auction.

7. "I like going up against the best from other schools, I like the mental stimulation, I like the battle of words," said the captain of the university debate team about the satisfaction she gets from debate competitions.

Exercise VII: Quote Stacking

Edit and trim the following to avoid quote stacking.

1. "I think that, ultimately, we will be facing a volatile situation with that bill," the senator from Wisconsin said. "We just cannot predict how our colleagues will vote based on party affiliation alone. There are currents and cross-currents, and conflicts of interest, and all kinds of special interest involved, and all sorts of other factors that will be a part of this. The whole picture is in flux."

2. "I really love coming to this area to perform," the comedian said. "The people are so cool and so tuned-in. It's gratifying to perform for an audience that seems to be so in synch

with my humor. It's actually a challenge to come up with new material that's going to play to their sophisticated level. But I'm up to the challenge. It keeps me sharp. And maybe I'll come up with some great new material for them. At least, I hope so."

3. "Taking pictures is something that spoke to my soul from the very beginning," the photographer from National Geographic said. "I just love the whole experience of going to faraway places, meeting new people, engaging new cultures, making new friends, taking hundreds and hundreds of photos, and coming back home and seeing the looks on people's faces when they see what new and exotic images I've brought to them. I also love that somebody pays me to do this. There's nothing else on the Earth I'd rather do than take pictures for National Geographic. I just cannot imagine a better job. Can you? I mean, can you, really?"

4. "It has become obvious that the city council is hostile to this agenda," the mayor said after last night's meeting. "When Councilman Jones made the motion to table my proposal pending further discussion and further research, it just drove a stake through my heart. We've discussed this thing thoroughly, I mean thoroughly, as much as you can discuss something, and I thought we had a consensus on it. Now this! I feel betrayed. I thought Jones was with the program. Now it seems that Mr. Jones is Mr. Judas."

5. "The suspect's car was searched by officers on the scene," the police sergeant told reporters. "We found two ounces of cocaine, two pounds of marijuana and several automatic weapons in the trunk of his car, a 1997 Ford Thunderbird. It is not possible at this time to estimate the street value of the drugs. It depends on the purity of the cocaine and the quality of the marijuana, I would guess. The automatic weapons are currently being checked for registration and ownership. The suspect is currently being held in county jail and is being questioned regarding several outstanding burglary, narcotics and homicide cases. I don't know if he has contacted a lawyer yet. I don't have the names of the arresting officers right now."

Exercise VIII: Simplifying Overloaded Sentences/Limiting Prepositional Phrases

Edit these passages so that there are no more than two or three prepositional phrases. You can elect to divide them into two simpler sentences.

1. In the morning after his landslide election victory over the longtime incumbent, the new governor called on his supporters to work hard for his anti-crime program for inner-city schools and to honor the outgoing administration for all its achievements in improving the state's economy and for bolstering its national image.

2. The university's new baseball coach will be looking for better leadership in the clubhouse and on the field, and wants players to be more concerned about team play, not individual achievements, and to be more appreciative of the school's traditions of sportsmanship and honor.

3. The representative from the high-tech firm from Austin, Texas, showed off a new DVD player/recorder from the company's new roster of products that has voice-recognition capabilities that will allow users to issue verbal commands to the DVD from remote locations.

4. The president's office, in consultation with the university legal counsel, has issued a campus-wide memo directing all academic departments to identify and delineate obvious and potential ethical issues arising from the new sex-discrimination legislation for possible discussion at the next meeting of the president's Committee for Gender Equity.

5. The exchange scholar from Mexico City has had little trouble adapting to his new environment, despite the demands from his soccer coach, the burden of having to communicate effectively in a foreign language, and the loneliness that comes with the separation from his family.

Exercise IX: Negative Constructions

Edit these passages to avoid excessive use of negatives.

1. The president vetoed a bill yesterday that would prevent states from imposing limits on the number of guns an individual can legally own.

2. The student council yesterday rejected a policy proposal that would have removed limits on the kinds of advertising that university-funded publications could refuse to accept.

3. The ambitious young politician said that he saw no need to express false modesty now, and that it would be "ridiculous" to decline the nomination.

4. The U.S. Supreme Court refused to hear a case involving an appellate court's overturning of a lower court decision upholding a ban on the sale of alcoholic beverages at the military academy's sporting events.

5. The blue-ribbon panel on police brutality declined to release its statement on officer non-conformity with federal laws, citing no need to publicize its findings until appropriate local and state authorities have been advised.

Exercise X: Coordinating and Subordinating Ideas

Edit these passages so that the words properly convey the relationships among ideas.

1. The teenage pianist from Indonesia was playing Beethoven masterpieces when she was 6 years old and will be performing "Moonlight Sonata" tonight at Madison Square Garden.

2. Most college graduates will have higher-paying jobs and greater job satisfaction than non-graduates, and are more likely to retire comfortably.

3. Henry Smith's wealthy cousin from Berlin got a Porsche for his birthday and wants to come to the United States to tour the highways in his new car.

4. Wendy Marcus was the sports editor of the school newspaper and had a bit of a conflict of interest because she was also the captain of the women's softball team.

5. Ken Luey's dream was to make the university chess team and within a year he found himself going to the international collegiate chess finals in Helsinki, Finland.

Exercise XI: Subordinating Ideas

Edit the following passages so that the main idea is not subordinated. Also edit for more effective sentence length and structure.

1. His father was a fan of the Beach Boys and his mother loved the Rolling Stones, so it is no

surprise that classic rock is also his passion, and, over the years, he has accumulated the largest collection in the nation of record albums from the 1950s to the 1980s, numbering more than 32,000 different items.

2. The screenwriter graduated from UCLA, finishing at the top of his class, and his contacts in his industry helped him get wonderful opportunities to write scripts for big-name stars like Sandra Bullock, Brad Pitt and Freddie Prinze Jr., including a screenplay that earned an Oscar nomination this week, just one year after he graduated from college.

3. Many young Cubans are listening to rap music, some Cuban farmers are starting to use alternative agricultural techniques, and some Cuban doctors are using laser technology, making it apparent that some segments of Cuban society are warming to ideas from the United States.

4. Raymond Washington's victory was predicted by every pundit and every editorial writer in the state, so it is no great surprise that he won election to his first major political office by a wide margin of votes, almost a 2-to-1 ratio, thus becoming the first person under the age of 45, the first Yale graduate and the first African-American to become mayor of this Southern city.

5. Although the scout noted that the tennis phenom's terrific backhand, booming serve and uncanny grace under pressure would be a windfall for the U.S. Davis Cup team, if she decided to join it, he added sympathetically that her defection yesterday in Seattle was "quite a loss" for the Russians.

Exercise XII: Time Elements

Edit the following sentences for better location of time indicators.

1. The editorial writer for the student newspaper yesterday learned that she'd won an award from the Society of Professional Journalists.

2. The fraternity brothers decided to take a road trip to Florida during spring break yesterday.

3. The program director of the student radio station on Tuesday said he would "fight the power" and defy the ban on explicit rap music.

4. Tomorrow the exchange students from Beijing will arrive on campus.

5. The club plans next week to stage a musical tribute to late singer/actress Aaliyah.

6. Legendary guitarist Carlos Santana gave yesterday a guest lecture in one of the university's ethnic studies classes.

7. The student body president said that he will not resign, despite the growing controversy, yesterday.

8. Last summer the young professor from Harvard earned his doctorate.

9. The labor crisis in Venezuela starting last week threatened to disrupt the world's oil supply.

10. He plans to buy today a new DVD player for his girlfriend.

Exercise XIII: Misplaced Modifiers

Edit the following for re-location of modifiers and for greater clarity.

1. Jerry Brown won re-election as mayor of Oakland today, whose voters clearly endorsed his political agenda.

2. The chairman of the Republican Party paid tribute to Georgia volunteers who campaigned for George W. Bush yesterday during ceremonies in Atlanta.

3. A local radio station today is running a Metallica marathon, one of the greatest bands in the history of heavy metal rock.

4. After a fight broke out during a game between the Knicks and the Lakers, the commissioner said he would fine the players who instigated the skirmish during a post-game meeting with team owners.

5. The submarine captain took on his first mission this week, which came much sooner than he expected.

6. She made history by becoming the first female cadet at the academy yesterday, which had been an all-male institution since its inception in 1899.

7. Today the supermodel from Argentina will fly to France to show off the latest fashions created by the quirky Italian designer in an international fashion show featuring several celebrity models.

8. The Picasso painting had been displayed in his San Francisco office since 1978, but was put in storage when he moved to San Marcos, Texas, where it remains.

Exercise XIV: Confusing Use of "And"

Edit the following for clarity.

1. The national conference of Elvis impersonators had been held in Las Vegas for the past 17 years, but last year promoters decided to commemorate Presley's birthday and bring it to Tupelo, Miss.

2. The activists from Lima held a rally in the campus plaza to call attention to Peru's economic woes and steep tuition increases for foreign students.

3. The psychology professor from Berkeley often reminisced about the 1960s, when he openly advocated resistance to the draft and freedom of speech.

4. He was an enthusiastic fan of the Dallas Cowboys and a football player during his student days at the University of Texas.

5. The police captain said that 30 marijuana plants and a carton of Twinkies stolen from the university's food services division were confiscated from the dorms yesterday.

Exercise XV: Editing for Style/Eliminating Clichés

Edit the clichés and overused expressions in these sentences. Find a different way to convey the intended meaning.

1. His instruments were not working, so the fighter pilot was blind as a bat in the thick fog.

2. He decided it was his turn to wreak havoc on his opponents.

3. The investigator was eyeing the suspect like a hawk.

4. She flashed a come-hither look at her admirers.

5. He showed his freshly minted diploma to his proud parents.

6. Even though he suffered great humiliation by their criticism, he decided to turn the other cheek.

7. When he heard he'd won the job, he was happy as a clam.

8. He was frozen like a deer caught in the headlights.

9. He'd had a difficult and busy week, so he needed some time to catch his breath.

10. He discerned that it was one of those Catch-22 situations.

11. The mayor seemed to have been caught in the crossfire of that controversy.

12. The chief executive officer knew she was in the catbird seat because she had the support of the board.

13. She had the intestinal fortitude to persist against all odds.

14. In the end, his frugal ways were penny-wise and pound-foolish.

15. He knew his proposal would have to take a back seat to more urgent matters.

16. The mayor threw a curve with her surprise proposal at the city council meeting.

17. She normally wore drab, conservative clothes, but at the party she was dressed to kill.

18. He was lacking in tact, and tended to shoot from the hip even when discussing delicate matters.

Exercise XVI: Grammar, Spelling, Punctuation, AP Style, Parallelism, Redundancy and Factual Accuracy

Edit the following.

1. The senate voted 51-to-49 to enact Pres. Bush's domestic security proposal. The bill now returns to the house, which passed the bill last week, for coordination and fine-tuning.

2. The City Manager of Austin, Tex., was the guest speaker at the San Francisco planning commission meeting last night.

3. There were several famous athletes of the past signing autographs at the card show last January, including Troy Aikman, Kenny "The Snake" Stabler, "Magic" Johnson and Deion "Prime Time" Sanders.

4. The library committee voted nine-to-seven to purchase more academic journals for the next school year. One of the affects of this vote is that students will have more copies of Journalism & Mass Communication Quarterly available to them.

5. According to city attorny Mike Smith, the ordenance passed by the city counsel last night was not un-Consitutional.

6. The professor knew that such manual-counting techniques for headlines, antiquated as they might seem, are required in most editing tests for fellowships and entry level jobs.

7. Either Canada or one of the Scandinavian countries are going to win the gold medal in that event, experts predict. The U.S., as well as host country, Germany, is considered a long shot.

8. Over one half of the classes offered next semester has a prerequesite. A student trying to enroll in JMC 322, for example will find that they can not unless they've already taken JMC 120.

9. Former Pittsburg Pirates great Willie Stargell died of a stroke at the age of sixty-one. He was remembered for his leadership, charisma and because he hit monumental homeruns.

10. Either the copy editors from the San Francisco Chronicle or the Assistant Managing Editor of the Los Angeles Times is judging the student entries from the west coast.

11. The East coast panel, which is composed of editors from the New York Times, Washington Post and the Miami Herald, say they are looking not only for adherence to A.P. style, they are also looking for good leads, crisp pacing and adroit-usage of quotes.

12. The 45 year old captain, a 21 year veteran of the Pittsburgh, PA police force, made plans to visit Buenos Aires for his winter vacation.

13. The eclectic public relations major applied for positions with the AFL-CIO, the U.N., the C.I.A, the BBC and the Boston Redsox baseball team.

14. Neither her parents nor her best friend were aware of her plans. Her and her fiancée had plane tickets for Rio de Janiero.

15. The senate sub-committee voted down the highway repair bill, tabled the monument renovation proposal and Senator Diane Feinstein's request for additional funds for coastline conservation was unanimously approved.

Exercise XVII: Putting It All Together

Edit the following story using all you've learned about editing for style.

It might come as a shock to many of the library users on campus that their records are susceptible to governmental handling.

The USA Patriot Act has become a major concern for library goers across the nation. The act allows the Federal Bureau of Investigation to gain access to records of business, medical history, education, and even what books people check out from libraries. The City College library is no exception.

Perhaps what is most disconcerting is the lack of notice the Patriot Act has received up until lately since being passed six weeks after September 11, 2001.

"The Patriot Act really scares me because I don't know exactly what it's all about." commented senior Richard Telesforo. "It seems like there were a lot of hasty decisions made after September 11."

Students of City College might want to take the time to read through the Library Privacy Policy, which is posted on the library's web site. "While a search warrant or court order is still required to obtain records the USA Patriot Act makes it much easier for the government to obtain both," the policy warns.

The policy also gives links to other sites on the web that summarize Section 215 (the section that deals with library records specifically) of the USA Patriot Act. Among the provisions affecting library confidentiality, FBI agents are allowed to obtain search warrants for anything "tangible," and the agent does *not* need to demonstrate "probable cause," according to Section 215. The agent need only claim the records are related to terrorism, intelligence activities or might contain information harmful to American interests abroad.

The libraries and librarians themselves are not allowed to disclose the existence of any warrants to anyone nor notify any library patrons that their records are being investigated, under penalty of law.

"We're under a gag order," said Wayne Jolley, Chair of Library Access Services Department at City College. Jolley takes an active and personal interest in the Patriot Act and maintains that librarians have been concerned with the act since its initial passing. He feels that the college has a unique advantage over the rest of society because of the environment of academic freedom.

"We have academic freedom on campus to discuss these political issues, and these advantages seem to be taken for granted," said Jolley. Milagros Moya, Information Services Chairperson of the City College library, expressed her hypothesis as to why more students aren't reacting to the Patriot Act.

"The name itself," Moya said, "sort of puts a tint on the act, it implies it's a good thing."

Moya also felt that "students should probably communicate with each other about what [the Patriot Act] is and what the impact is. The student may not be aware how much it affects them."

Greg Oribado, a student here at City College, became visibly rattled when told of the Patriot Act and its many ramifications.

"That does it," he muttered, and started off in the general direction of Washington, D.C.

At least one student, however, is taking a different perspective on the issue.

"It's kind of cool that there really are these murky, insidious depths to our government," said Isabel Garcia, vice president of the Literary Elite campus club.

"It reminds me of books like 1984, with Big Brother watching. I'm going to go borrow some really subversive books from the library and see if anything happens."

CHAPTER 5
Editing for Accuracy and Fairness

Exercise I: Popular Culture Trivia

Match the actor/actress with the movie.

1. Vanilla Sky __   **a.** Dennis Hopper

2. A Streetcar Named Desire __   **b.** Denzel Washington

3. Giant __   **c.** Marlon Brando

4. The Misfits __   **d.** Marilyn Monroe

5. Blue Velvet __   **e.** John Wayne

6. Bill and Ted's Excellent Adventure __   **f.** Jodie Foster

7. Windtalkers __   **g.** Tom Hanks

8. Taxi Driver __   **h.** Sean Connery

9. To Sir, With Love __   **i.** Sidney Poitier

10. Beverly Hills Cop __   **j.** Tom Cruise

11. Apollo 13 __   **k.** Natalie Wood

12. Hurricane __   **l.** Bruce Lee

13. Goldfinger __   **m.** Lou Diamond Phillips

14. Dog Day Afternoon __   **n.** Whoopi Goldberg

15. Saturday Night Fever __   **o.** Jennifer Lopez

16. Romeo Must Die __   **p.** Jimmy Stewart

17. Splendor in the Grass __   **q.** John Travolta

18. Sister Act __   **r.** Al Pacino

19. La Bamba __   **s.** Keanu Reeves

20. Enter the Dragon __   **t.** Arnold Schwarzenegger

21. Harry Potter and the Sorcerer's Stone __   **u.** James Dean

22. Conan the Destroyer __   **v.** Nicholas Cage

23. Back to Bataan __   **w.** Renee Zellweger

24. Nurse Betty __   **x.** Jet Li

25. It's a Wonderful Life __   **y.** Daniel Radcliffe

26. Selena __   **z.** Eddie Murphy

Exercise II: Sports Trivia

Match the athlete with his or her sport.

1. Allan Iverson __   **16.** Joe Montana __   **a.** figure skating

2. Barry Bonds __   **17.** Andre Agassi __   **b.** hockey

3. Wayne Gretzky __   **18.** Yao Ming __   **c.** football

4. Sheryl Swoopes __   **19.** Mario Andretti __   **d.** basketball

5. Tara Lipinski __   **20.** Billie Jean King __   **e.** baseball

6. Bjorn Borg __   **21.** Barry Zito __   **f.** cycling

7. Lance Armstrong __   **22.** George Foreman __   **g.** auto racing

8. Ty Cobb __   **23.** Wilt Chamberlain __   **h.** tennis

9. Nancy Kerrigan __   **24.** Lou Gehrig __   **i.** boxing

10. Emmitt Smith __   **25.** Muhammad Ali __

11. Willie Mays __   **26.** Chris Evert __

12. Mario Lemieux __   **27.** Anna Kournikova __

13. Jeff Gordon __   **28.** Eric Lindros __

14. Lennox Lewis __   **29.** Michael Vick __

15. Venus Williams __   **30.** Eddie George __

Exercise III: Cultural, Historical and Geographical References

Correct the factual inaccuracies in the following sentences. (Use reference books and Internet sources to get the right information.)

1. In his first movie, "Rebel Without a Cause," James Dean played a restless teen trying to find meaning in his life.

2. The Beatles' first live appearance on American TV was on "The Ed Sullivan Show" in 1963.

3. Honolulu, the capital of Hawaii, lies on the island of Maui, the second largest of the state's islands.

4. Thomas Jefferson, the founder of the Democratic Republican Party and one of the drafters of the Declaration of Independence, was the second president of the United States.

5. After John F. Kennedy's assassination, his profile replaced Franklin Roosevelt's on the 50-cent piece in U.S. coinage.

6. Three of Marvel Comics' most popular superheroes are Spider-Man, Captain America and Batman.

7. The Philippines is the only Caribbean nation that is predominantly Catholic.

8. Sumeria, the world's oldest civilization, was located in the area that is now known as Israel.

9. The first Super Bowl, played in 1966, featured the Green Bay Packers and the Oakland Raiders.

10. The only U.S. presidents to have been impeached are Andrew Johnson, Richard Nixon and Bill Clinton.

11. Russian philosopher Karl Marx outlined his vision for socialist economics and class struggle in his book "Das Kapital."

12. The San Francisco Giants appeared in the World Series in 1954, 1961, 1989 and 2002.

13. Elvis Presley, recognized by many as the greatest rock 'n' roll star of all time, was born in Memphis, Tenn.

14. William Shakespeare, who emerged in the 15th century as the greatest of England's dramatists, showed a brilliant comic touch in "As You Like It."

15. Leonard Nimoy, who played Dr. Spock in the classic "Star Trek" series, also directed one of the movies based on the TV show.

16. Earl Warren, former chief justice of the United States, was attorney general of California when President Eisenhower appointed him to the high court.

17. During World War II, America joined with its allies to fight the Axis powers, led by Germany, Japan and the Soviet Union.

18. Saturn, the largest planet in our solar system, is the sixth farthest from the sun and features bright equitorial rings.

19. The first Europeans to land on North American soil were the crew of Norman explorer Leif Ericsson, who sailed west from Greenland around the year 1000.

20. The original members of the Beatles were John Lennon, Paul McCartney, George Harrison, Ringo Starr and Stu Sutcliffe.

Exercise IV: Geographical Accuracy

Edit the following for spelling, wording and geographical accuracy.

1. The senator's tour of South America included stops in Bolivia, Columbia, Chile, Ecuador and Costa Rica.

2. His favorite cities in the West are San Francisco, Las Vegas, Salt Lake City and San Antonio.

3. The travel writer from Wyoming had never been to the Phillipines, and he didn't speak the Filipino language.

4. Her favorite states in the South Atlantic region are Florida, Georgia, Alabama, Maryland and Delaware.

5. He spent the summer of 1993 traveling through the Soviet Union.

6. Her cousin from Azerbaijan did not bring any Azerbaijanian artifacts with her when she visited the United States.

7. Travelers to Rio de Janeiro are advised to learn Spanish, the national language of Brazil.

8. The adventurous traveler wanted to go island-hopping in Asia, so he made plans to visit Japan, Vietnam, Singapore and the Philippines.

9. She came from Australia, the smallest continent in the world. So she set her sights on Europe, the largest.

10. The representatives from Scandinavia included delegates from Sweden, Norway, Iceland, Germany and the Netherlands.

11. Afghanistan, a landlocked country, shares borders with Tajikistan, Turkmenistan, Uzbekistan, Iran, Iraq, Pakistan and China.

Exercise V: Geographical References

CASE STUDY #1

You are the travel editor for a large metropolitan daily. You allow your writers to use first person references because you like to have "literary adventure" pieces in your section. You receive this story submission from one of your favorite freelancers. Make a list of the editing tasks you have ahead of you.

I was about to be robbed. I was in Ojo de Agua in the newly formed territory of Estado de Mexico. Formerly a hacienda, this bustling enclave of 25,000 still has some of its indigenous and colonial charm, yet it now rests in the shadow of the looming immensity of the cosmopolitan La Ciudad (Mexico City). Ojo de Agua is on the verge of being subsumed, and was already exhibiting the signs of near-exponential growth. I was about to have my yogurt and Doritos stolen by six 13-year old punks. They encircled me. The taller one with his nose pierced like a bull's lobbed a soccer ball at me.
"You buy," said the bull.
"*No entiendo* (I don't understand)," I replied.
"Give us money," said bleached hair.
"The Aurora *mercado* has it, you can have the yogurt."

They made no move to accept the bag held out to them so I pushed my way through the circle and didn't look back, figuring that might indicate a challenge. They didn't move, but I kept walking. At that moment, I wished more than anything to be safe in the arms of the mountain, the chill of her icy breath on my face. Iztaccihuatl (Ixta), where I would be in two days, was nearly three miles above the city and its thieves.

Ixta and her lover Popocatepetl (Popo) rest some 50 miles south of the sprawl of Mexico City. La Ciudad sits a mile above sea level but Ixta and Popo rise above its tallest buildings by some 12,000 feet. I had hoped to be standing on El Pecho, the summit and breast of the sleeping Ixta, by noon. In the pre-dawn dark illuminated by the headlights of my father-in-law Lazaro's car, I shouldered my 30-pound pack, complete with ice axe, plastic boots, crampons, food, water, Diamox (in case of altitude sickness) and warm clothes in the pre-dawn dark. I had to walk an extra two miles to La Jolla, the beginning of the route, as the road got too rough for the Dodge Spirit.

The last words I heard that morning were Lazaro's thickly accented demand. "You be careful!"

The darkness kept my thoughts anchored to distant realities. The peak, still hidden, would not pull my attention for several hours until I hit the rock and snow bands. According to legend, Ixta was an Aztec princess whose father forbade marriage to her lover Popocatepetl, who was of the lower, warrior class. Word was sent to Ixta that he had died in battle. Hearing this, she died of grief. Popo, very much alive, returned to his love and carried her to the mountains and laid her there to rest for eternity. He stayed by her side and became the active volcano that today threatens some 25 million (including all the inhabitants of La Ciudad) who continue to make their homes at his feet. Even today, many view him as protector, and refuse to leave even when his coughing gets aggravated, which happens with an expected regularity, like the waxing of the moon.

The day before my ascent I drove up from Amecameca with my wife and her family to Paso de Cortez. This year like the last five there was very little snow, and despite it being midwinter, it was clear and 75 degrees. At the climber's hut, we learned from the snow-goggled caretaker that Popo had been heating up considerably. We were at 12,000 feet, yet he said when it storms, the snow doesn't stick. I asked him if he was scared.

"I can't live shaking in my boots my whole life," he said, attempting his most convincing laugh. He told us the slopes of Popo and its summit had been off limits to climbers and everyone else for several years now, rendering the once bustling resort of Tlamacas, just a couple miles up the road, a ghost town. "The government believes it is too dangerous to be near the mountain," he said. A month before I arrived, a film crew had illegally hiked the shoulder of Popo to get footage for a documentary on volcanoes. As if in response, Popo coughed out projectiles that killed a cameraman.

Hernando Cortez had his experience with Popo half a millennium before. An amazing tactician, Cortez launched his surprise attack on the Aztecs by heading through the saddle between Popo and Ixta that now bears his name. The Aztecs would not have suspected anyone would come through the mountains, especially not an army that had never been through the treacherous pass. Cortez was able to slip through to the back door of the Aztec Empire before any real alarm could be raised. On his way he stopped at the shoulder of Popo, who was angrily coughing out smoke and pyroclastics. He sent some of his troops up for the first known summit bid. They negotiated the steep ice at the 18,000-foot high caldera and lowered a man in, via many ropes knotted together. He quickly loaded his pack with sulfur-rich stones, and amazingly was not overcome by the fumes. They pulled him out with a fresh supply of sulfur needed for their guns and artillery.

On the day I climbed Ixta, Popo again exhaled large clouds of threatening smoke, and from Los Pies (The Feet), I had an amazing view of the puffing cinder cone. To the distant north the countless red, yellow, and white twinkles of La Ciudad were being snuffed out one by one as the morning got brighter. The full moon was ready to slip away, and like an old man drawing his final breath, was poised at the edge of the world. I wasn't doing much better, breathing quite heavily, and not convinced I could summit with the 40 pounds on my back. I had started taking antibiotics a few days before, having contracted Montezuma's Revenge, and that was adding to my debilitating fatigue.

I had only hiked for a few hours and gained only a couple thousand feet in altitude, yet I had never been so tired. I would stop on the trail and pass out for one, two, five-minutes maybe. Then I would wobble a hundred feet further in my hypoxic (oxygen starved) state, fall over and sleep again. I had read too many stories of climbers not being able to wake up when this happened, so I decided to ditch my pack at Las Rodillas (The Knees), and attempt the summit without the extra 30 pounds. I was now just below the summit ridgeline and because there were just traces of snow that were easily avoided, I left everything but my camera off the side of the trail. At over 16,000 feet I was sure it would be safe. Leaving one's pack while making the final summit push is common practice in the mountaineering world.

Over the first knob of rock I passed the Buenos Aires hut and party of Mexican climbers that had spent the night there. I then chose to follow the steepest part of the ridgeline as it was free of snow. After an hour of picking the line of least resistance up the steep rock band, I made myself believe I was in sight of the breast, El Pecho, and decided that that would be enough. I sat next to a huge metal cross among the ghosts of Ixta. I had already passed a couple of dozen crosses coming up the steep rock band. At least I made it further than they had. I was so exhausted I couldn't enjoy the view, but noted that La Malinche, another tall volcano, was a mere pimple on the brown skin of high desert to the south. Further on, over a hundred miles distant, I spotted the tallest peak in Mexico Citlatepetl, or Pico de Orizaba, as the Spanish chose to call it. What pulled my attention first were the dazzling white arms, like that of an albino starfish; they were snowfields that stretched down the cinder cone.

Several hundred feet below my perch on the rocky ridge, I could make out the twisted wreckage of an airplane. Given the remnants of past disasters, I reasoned it was time to leave before I added myself to the number of casualties. My head felt as if my brain was a balloon being blown up inside my head. Everyone deteriorates at altitude and some more quickly than others. After a few steps I realized that I could no longer put total faith in my balance. It was time to get down, fast. Statistically, mountaineering is the most deadly sport on the planet (more than 300 a year will die in the mountains), and I really didn't want to add to these staggering figures. I delicately negotiated the 1,000 or so near-vertical feet of the loose rock band, found the trail, and felt a little more relaxed.

When I got to the spot where I had left my pack, it was gone, spirited away by the mountain goddess. I was shocked. The $500 in lost equipment seemed immaterial, as the terrain wouldn't get me, but without food, water, and the Diamox (prescription drugs for high altitude) I had brought for just such an emergency, I would eventually just shut down, having no strength to move. My head was now pounding intensely. I was altitude sick and wanted to get down, but now I was too pissed to think straight, and decided that the Buenos Aires hut I had passed just above, with the party of Mexican climbers, must be where my pack was. I stumbled back over the brown hydra-head of stone with fists clenched, and from the door of the hut I accused them all, in broken Spanish, of being thieves, and said I would die without my pack.

"*Se robaron tu mochila*? (They stole your pack?)" said the closest one, as he grabbed his archaic wooden ice axe and held it to his chest, blocking the door.

At that moment, having invited it, I was certain I would die.

"*Vamos, vamos!*" (Let's go!) he shouted.

He pointed at me, then to his eyes to make me understand we would look for the thieves. Who can argue with a man wielding an ice axe? I only had a camera to defend myself so I let him do the directing. He led me away from the hut and down the mountain by a steeper trail I had not seen before, more to the west. I staggered on, trying to keep up, but kept out of range of his axe. He was obviously well acclimated, and although not tall he was barrel-chested and extremely fit, not even registering fatigue. I felt like a battered lizard being toyed with by a cocksure cat. I thought of Trotsky. With every faltering step I remembered a stupid mistake I had made that day. Any minute now he would have my jacket and camera too, and I would be neatly stuffed in one of the mountain's innumerable rock crevices. After a few minutes of lung-bursting sprinting down steep pumice sand, I figured out his diabolical plan: he would wait until I had an aneurysm and did myself in of "natural" causes. But as we reached the main trail again a scary thing happened. He suddenly stopped.

"This is it," I thought. I wasn't falling over quickly enough for his liking. He let his arm open wide like a pitcher winding up for a fastball, only he had a sharp axe instead. I stood motionless, knowing exactly what the raccoon on the double-yellow thinks when eyes lock on the flood of halogen. Then there were voices, sweet voices from just behind him. Nervously looking back, he lowered the axe and told me he would run ahead to catch up with the thieves.

My saviors rounded the bend—a young Mexican couple from La Ciudad, doing a short day hike to Los Pies. After hearing my tale of woe they offered me some of their water and a chocolate bar. "You are very lucky," they insisted in English. I had to agree, yet I was still at 15,000 feet. I had to hurry down, so I said goodbye and headed down the trail. The pressure in my head was a big clue (poor decision-making being another) that I was suffering the early signs of HACE, High Altitude Cerebral Edema, and my head really would explode if I couldn't make it to a much lower elevation very soon. My dumb luck would be for naught.

Finally I made it back to La Jolla. Mr. Axe was there, grinning. He had met up with some more friends. They offered me a ride. I lied and told them I had a ride coming. They waited around some more to make sure, and thankfully the young city couple made it down to save me a second time. They drove me the six miles to the Paso De Cortez, where I would meet Lazaro.

Three days later, down at a survivable altitude in Ojo de Agua, I still had the throbbing headache and got winded just climbing the stairs of my father-in-law's house, but I felt safe from thieves. It helped that they had bars on the windows and broken glass cemented to the top of the high walls that boxed in the house. I stayed inside, recovering slowly, which gave me ample time to watch the Mexican news with my wife. The price of the tortilla was up, signifying imminent recession. The average wage in Mexico was hovering at just $4 a day. Popo was angry again.

It was time for me to go home.

Exercise VI: Geographical and Historical References

CASE STUDY #2

You are an international news editor for a big-time newspaper, and one of your staffers turns in this breaking story about a local scholar who'd been kidnapped in the Philippines. Make a list of the editing concerns you'd have with this story.

After about a period of two weeks, Joseph Sandoval will return home to Reno, on Saturday, Nov. 10 after being kidnapped by a terrorist group in the southern Philippine islands. He is currently staying at U.S. Embassy facilities in Davao City on the island of Mindanao, and after being interviewed by Philippine and American authorities in Manila.

"I am pleased that this ordeal is over," said Sandoval, a full-time faculty member at the University of Nevada. "I just want to go home now."

Sandoval was first reported abducted on Oct. 22, and was discovered by members of the Philippine military tied to a tree in a remote jungle area in Jolo, the biggest island in the southern Philippines. They reported that military members were notified in advance by cellular phone contact, and that no ransom or explanation was received by the rebel terrorists.

The rebel group has claimed to be the Abu Sayyaf and is an Islamic splinter group off the Al-Harakatul Islamia, also having ties with Osama bin Ladin. The Abu Sayyaf, meaning "Bearer of the Sword", is seeking funds for their small army of roughly 700 young Islamic radicals, and mainly finances their operations through piracy, robbery, and ransom kidnappings.

April 12, 2000, Jeffery Craig Schilling, an American Muslim convert, was abducted by the same rebel group while he was visiting their Jolo Island stronghold. On Aug. 22, 2000, Schilling was released as hostage and the Philippine government reported the ransom paid by Libya.

In the extent to recover arms for the active fighters, Libya has paid off ransoms in the past to further endorse Islamic fundamentalism in the southern Philippines.

"Sandoval was involved in research for him and the university while staying in Mindanao," said Peter Schmidt, the assistant media coordinator out of the San Francisco U.S. State Department. "He will be returning soon in good health with important information for authorities."

Along with interviews with the Philippine and American authorities in Manila, the U.S. State Department and FBI have ongoing investigations on the current terrorism situation in the southern Philippines. The rebel group originally demanded a two million dollar ransom, but after negotiations by Philippine and American authorities the Islamic radicals released Sandoval.

"Nov. 1, was the last communication made with federal negotiators after the rebel group let Sandoval free," said Joseph Merriweather, a deputy information officer and spokesman for the university. "Sandoval was looking at indoctrination rituals by the rebel terrorists for both his Native American studies class and upcoming book."

After the last contact was made with the rebel group the Philippine government reported the hostage released in a remote jungle in Jolo. He was reported dehydrated and undernourished but in good health overall with only minor scrapes.

"Joe Sandoval just got in a little too deep, analyzing initiation rituals in the rebel group," said Maurice D'Angelo, a friend and co-worker with Sandoval at the university. "After he got his grant from the university he was eager to find new information for his book."

D'Angelo also noted that Sandoval probably found interesting similarities in the Islamic rebels along with Native American Tribes. Sandoval will be finishing his book in the next four months, and will probably get it published sometime next year, said D'Angelo.

Exercise VII: Cultural Sensitivity

Edit the following sentences to eliminate insensitive racial and cultural references. If the sentence is fine as it is, explain why.

1. The drill team was not organized, and its presentation resembled a Chinese fire drill.

2. The chairman of the Black Student Caucus strutted offstage after his presentation.

3. The scent of tacos, enchiladas and other Mexican foods filled the air inside the Hernandez home.

4. There were mostly Latin and black players on that team, and they played with a lot of emotion.

5. He knew his girlfriend's family lived in a trailer park, so he tried to keep the conversation simple.

6. Being from a hard-working Jewish family, he knew the value of a dollar.

7. Refugees from former communist countries just can't seem to get enough of capitalism.

8. He didn't have the effete manner and upper-class attitudes of a Harvard graduate.

9. His friends did not approve of his Filipino girlfriend because they believed the practice of courting mail-order brides was not respectable.

10. He knew it would be a tough negotiation with his ruthless Japanese colleague.

11. The German people, who are used to regimentation and harsh punishment, readily accepted the new orders.

12. Being from a Latvian family, he appreciated a good, strong drink.

Exercise VIII: Geographical References and Cultural Sensitivity

CASE STUDY #3

Two weeks after Elisabeth Ramek arrived in Israel, a bomb went off in downtown Tel Aviv.

A Palestinian suicide bomber had joined a line of mostly Russian revelers outside a nightclub called the Dolphinarium, and detonated himself. Twenty-one people, most between the ages of 14 and 19, died from the blast, and 120 others were maimed or wounded. A friend of Ramek's worked as a guard at the club.

"He told me he saw body parts flying," she said quietly.

Ramek, a student at Michigan State University, spent three months working and living in the danger zone by choosing to visit Tel Aviv, the cultural, financial and commercial heart of Israel.

Ramek was not alone in her quest to explore this burgeoning city. Newsweek magazine has listed Tel Aviv as one of the top 10 cities in the world to which young people migrate. According to the magazine, it is the country's most expensive city and has become the center of high-tech growth almost by default, since it is the only Israeli metropolis that operates on the same 24-hour schedule as the tech industry.

An experienced waitress, Ramek was quickly hired upon her arrival in Tel Aviv. One of her jobs was at a travelers' blues bar on the beach, next door to the U.S. Embassy. As the waves of the Mediterranean Ocean crashed against the sand and the blues wept from the instruments, Ramek served drinks to people in search of relaxation. In Israel, people have learned to relax, to remain stoic, even as imminent danger lurks. In Israel, bombings and other kinds of violence are reported daily.

Ramek recalled one day when she attended a wedding. The celebration continued even though the sound of automatic gunfire crackled in the distance.

"It was the most incredible thing," she said, to see all that happiness when people were killing each other just a few miles away.

On another occasion, terrorists set off a bomb in a business district of Jerusalem. When Ramek visited the area a couple of days later, everything seemed calm. Everything seemed like it was business as usual.

"I saw people walking around as if nothing was wrong," Ramek recalled.

When asked if she was afraid of entering this kind of environment by herself as a young American woman, her face relaxed into a calm smile.

"My fears aren't about life or death. Everything's working out the way it's supposed to," she said.

The suicide bombing at the Dolphinarium intensified already fierce pressure on Prime Minister Ariel Sharon for retaliatory air strikes, assasination and other attacks on Palestinian targets, which had been suspended under a policy of restraint for two weeks.

In the wake of the September 11 terrorist attacks on the U.S., Americans have been horrified by images of businesspeople jumping from the burning World Trade Center towers. To most, the carnage is incomprehensible. Ramek learned in Israel that what Americans consider "terrorism" is a way of life for many people.

"Israeli people are incredibly strong and brave. They're very outspoken and honest in general; they've learned how to cope," she explained.

Instead of cowering under the shadow of violence, citizens of Israel abide by stricter security regulations to help combat the threat of violence. Based on her experience, Ramek believes it would have been impossible for the suicide hijackers who attacked the U.S. to board an Israeli flight.

After the bombing at the Dolphinarium this summer, Ramek's dad called to offer her a plane ticket to anywhere else in the world is she left the turmoil of Israel.

She stayed.

"Fear has its place and can help keep us safe, but it can also inhibit us from life and fulfilling our dreams," Ramek said.

"I learned from the people I met in Israel that we should make the most of our time here, and do our best to live our lives without fear."

Respond briefly to the following.

1. Make a list of the things you, as editor, need to verify.

2. How would you evaluate the tone of this piece?

3. Is there enough historical and cultural context?

4. Is the use of only one source in this story acceptable? What other sources could be contacted? What information could be developed by other sources?

5. In the fifth paragraph there is a reference to Newsweek magazine's recognition of Tel Aviv's attractiveness to young travelers. Is the technique of citing another publication's work acceptable here? Is there any other way we could've developed this information?

6. Are there any errors in AP style, grammar, spelling and punctuation?

7. Are there any other important issues raised by this article?

Exercise IX: Comparing Newspaper Coverage

Find a widely covered story and compare how three newspapers (local, regional and national) covered it.

Exercise X: Balance

Situation: One of your reporters writes goes on a tree-sitting mission with a group of eco-activists and comes back with a first-person account. His article contains the following passage. Make a list of issues you, as editor, face with this passage.

From the top of the ridge where we now stood we could see the devastation that clear-cutting a forest causes. We decided that this is where the tree-sit would take place. An entire side of a hill looked as though it had been carpet-bombed. Nothing remained except piles of brush and lonely stumps. The site covered acres. Smaller trees and those deemed not profitable to cut gathered in twos and threes to look out over the dead.

The wind, which before had been slowed by the trees, now howled up around us, bringing with it the smells of trucks and sawdust. "Apocalyptic" seemed the only word that fit.

Mankind will never cease to amaze me. For all its advancements, it has the overwhelming ability to destroy beautiful things. We picked our way from the piles of brush and the forgotten tree stumps to the edge of the clear cut, near section 9. If the lumber company continued to disobey the court order, this is where they would come next.

Situation: A reporter submits this story about race hatred in the community. Make a list of issues you have with this passage.

Ravi Iyer, a student of East Indian descent, experienced an unpleasant encounter at his job one day after the September 11, 2001, terrorist attacks on the World Trade Center.

Iyer was working the register at the liquor store that late afternoon when a young man came in to buy a soda. As the customer approached the counter, he looked Iyer straight into his eyes and said, "I hate greens like you," referring to the green cards non-American citizens must have to be admitted into the United States.

"You ragheads are the ones who messed up our country," the customer said to Iyer. He remembers remaining professional and assisting the customer, despite the strong racist sentiment he expressed.

"You shouldn't be saying these things. It is not my fault," Iyer responded.

Anger and sadness filled his eyes when Iyer recalled what the disturbed customer said as he left: "If we go to war, I am going to come in here and shoot you." While making his statement the young man cast his hand as if it were a gun and pointed toward Iyer and said, "Bang, bang, bang."

This is just one of many incidents involving racial hatred that happened after the attacks on the World Trade Center. This situation further supports the fact that social injustice still lingers in our society. The question that arises is: Why do racism, bigotry, and discrimination still reign, forcefully or subtly, in our country?

Situation: A reporter submits this article about a campaign exchange by an incumbent senator and his challenger. What issues would you face with this passage?

The senator beamed at the crowd of supporters, who chanted "six more years, six more years" for several minutes while waving a sea of American flags.

Then, speaking directly to the issue of patriotism, the senator declared in a loud voice that he supported the new anti-terrorist legislation, an issue his opponent has wavered on.

"I love my country," the senator said. "I hate terror. It's pretty simple. My opponent, the esteemed mayor, doesn't seem to get it."

Mayor Smith initially did not return phone calls seeking comment, but said later in front of a small crowd at a shopping mall that he didn't agree with the senator's characterization of him.

"I haven't wavered at all," the mayor said. "I, uh, still think that there are important civil rights issues that need to be addressed before we rush to any judgment on that legislation."

When told of Smith's response, the senator said that the mayor was "a fool."

CHAPTER 6
Legal and Ethical Issues for Editors

Exercise I: Vocabulary

Write brief definitions for the following.

1. Libel

2. Slander

3. Invasion of privacy

4. Shield law

5. Sunshine law

6. Copyright infringement

7. Fair comment and criticism

8. Actual malice

9. Reckless disregard for the truth

10. Public figure

11. Freedom of Information Act

12. Chilling effect

13. Absolute privilege

Exercise II: Landmark Cases

Tell briefly the significance of New York Times vs. Sullivan (1964).

Exercise III: Freedom of Information

Situation: You want to find air-safety records about a particular airline and a specific airport, but your primary sources have refused to disclose the information. Give a step-by-step narrative on how to obtain what you need using the Freedom of Information Act.

Exercise IV: Applications

Indicate whether each statement is true or false.

_____ **1.** If a contested statement in a news story cannot be proven false, then a libel suit will be thrown out.

_____ **2.** If a plaintiff is a public figure, then a libel suit will be thrown out in all circumstances.

_____ **3.** If a rock critic writes an opinion piece about a rock star's ragged appearance, saying he "looked like he hadn't showered in about a month," the critic could lose a libel suit.

_____ **4.** If a columnist were to misstate a fact and seriously damage the reputation of someone, he can always invoke the "opinion defense" and not lose a libel suit.

_____ **5.** Israeli prime minister Ariel Sharon won a $50 million libel suit against Time because a jury found that the story about him was false, and the reporter knew that the information was false beforehand.

_____ **6.** Inserting the words "alleged" or "allegedly" in crime cases always protects the reporter against libel suits.

_____ **7.** Courts consider headlines and stories two components of a whole, thus you will not libel someone in a headline if you qualify the information in the story.

_____ **8.** Implying that someone is sexually loose does not put a story in a libel "danger zone" because the world has become more sexually enlightened in recent decades.

_____ **9.** Stating that someone is a member of a known hate group could make a reporter vulnerable to a libel suit.

_____ **10.** Truth is always a defense in cases involving libel or invasion of privacy.

_____ **11.** When illustrating a story about prostitution, it would be OK to use a picture of any provocatively dressed person walking down a city street, as long as that person's identity is not discernible.

_____ **12.** The public and the media have the right to attend government meetings, including those that involve personnel matters and labor negotiating sessions.

Exercise V: When Reporters Break the Law

You are the lifestyle editor of a major metropolitan newspaper located in the San Francisco Bay Area. One of your reporters turns in a first-person story about his adventure on a clandestine tree-sitting mission containing the following passage. What issues would you, as editor, face?

I walked back up to where the guide for that night's mission was standing. I told him I had no idea exactly what I was getting myself into. He told me, "None of us do, but at the very least, maybe we can save some trees."

The first thing I noticed, when I was deep in the woods at midnight, was how natural it felt to be there. We were walking along a privately owned logging road, the dirt packed hard from the use of so many bulldozers and logging trucks. The moon, high above us in her bed, filtered down softly through the immense canopy of old growth Douglass Fir. The wind blew slight and heavy with the scent of pine and earth. The four of us walked in pairs, separated by 20 yards.

This, I was told, was so that in the morning the security detail could not follow our tracks and find out how many had been out there that night. After the arrests that morning, the group members were eager to get someone up in a tree, to halt any further logging.

We walked on in silence. The fear we felt that at any moment we could be stopped by roving bands of security guards, not only heightened our awareness, but also made us all paranoid. We were trespassing on private land, after all. And the tree that Raven would be sitting in was on private property, as well.

Extra questions:

1. If this story is published and the property owners complain, what would you do? What would you do if the police say they want to talk with the reporter?

2. What if authorities ask to see the reporter's notes, or ask the reporter to provide the identities of the group? What would you do?

3. Suppose the owners of the property are regular advertisers in your newspaper. How would you handle this? Should this be a factor in the decisions you make about this story?

Exercise VI: Confidential Sources

CASE STUDY #1

For this exercise, please refer to the story in Chapter 5 about the professor who was kidnapped in the Philippines. After the story has been edited and prepared for publication in the next day's paper, the reporter hands you two memos that were sent to him by "Raul," a secret source he has in the U.S. State Department. They read as follows:

Memo #1 from Raul:

Dear _____

There's more to this story than what the State Dept. is letting on publicly.

I'll tell you the following information knowing that you will not use my name. I know you will absolutely not share this information with anyone at this time, nor will you speak about this publicly. Do you promise? I trust you. Of course, you can go ahead and do what you want with this information in terms of writing your story. Just don't attribute anything to me.

Here's the story: The professor was there not just working on a book, he was doing some surveillance for the U.S. government. He was trying to determine where other Western hostages were being kept. He and D'Angelo and others have links to counterterrorist forces working in the southern Philippines. They were trying to coordinate an effort with U.S. intelligence and the Philippine military, but the plan went afoul when someone in Abu got wind of it. That's when Sandoval was kidnapped.

I don't know how you'll be able to use this information, since you cannot attribute it to me. And I seriously doubt that you'll get anyone from State to comment on it. I just thought you might want to know the real scoop so you don't go running around blind.

Have a nice day!

RAUL

Memo #2 from Raul:

Hello! You're really onto something, aren't you? I don't know if you'll be able to use it since you only have it from an anonymous source (me). But it's true! Sandoval and D'Angelo are working for us. They take money from us. They take direction from us. But you'll never get them to admit it. They're sworn to secrecy. Also, you'll never get Sandoval or any of those suits in the bureaucracy to confirm this information. They'll issue a flat-out "no comment." But that tells you a lot, doesn't it?

There is a bigger issue here, though: that of the public interest. You probably are aware that if you use this information in a newspaper article, you might be compromising any covert operations we may have going on in the Philippines. This could very well compromise the safety of a lot of people if it gets out that some American intellectuals are acting as espionage agents for the U.S. Don't you think? Don't you think the public interest would be served in a bigger and better way if you just keep this information to yourself, and don't put it in your story? Search your soul, my friend.

Since we go a long way back, you deserve to know the truth.

Here's the story: Sandoval was indeed on a research mission for a book, but he was also on a spy mission (as I told you before). He got some secret funding from the U.S. government to cover some of his expenses, i.e., for bribes he was paying out to some of the locals in Mindanao to get inside info on Abu. Well, word got around real quick that there was an American handing out fistfuls of U.S. green to get access to the Abu. Let's say that JG wasn't as discreet as he should've been. A couple of terrible guys apparently heard the news and got to Sandoval and took him away at gunpoint. Automatic weapons. AK-47's. Were the abductors Abu members? They claimed they were. I'm convinced they were. Some of the eggheads here at State aren't so sure, though, because some of these captors' methods weren't consistent with past Abu methods. Real crude. Not at all sophisticated. It could be that these were teenage fringe Abu members who were trying to turn a quick buck and/or get some fast notoriety. Maybe it was part of their indoctrination ritual to join an Abu cell – to hook up with the Big Boys. Who knows for sure? I don't. But my best guess is that they were Abu members or wanna-be members or guys who were being indoctrinated. When the heat was turned on, they wilted and went crying back to their mommies. If you report that they were Abu members, that wouldn't be 100 percent correct. If you report that they are believed to be Abu members or Abu sympathizers, that would be closer to the truth.

As always, RAUL

Respond briefly to the following.

1. Should we use any of this information in the story, knowing that we'll probably beat all the competition with the "inside" scoop?

2. Discuss the confirmation and verification issues you face with this story.

3. How would you approach government officials with this information?

4. What factors would go into your decision to develop and eventually publish this information?

Exercise VII: Protecting Sources/Invasion of Privacy

CASE STUDY #2

Situation: You are the managing editor of your newspaper. The city editor asks you to read over this story about a prostitute.

THE WORLD'S OLDEST PROFESSION

"I want to work with young people and show them this isn't the way," Penny said. "As it is, if one of these young girls is beaten or robbed, we can't go to the cops. They just look at us and say, 'What do you want us to do? You're a prostitute.'"

Imagine yourself walking the streets of Old Town Eureka at 9 p.m. looking for tricks to fill your pockets so you can go to your drug connection and get another fix—just to get you through the next day. Hard to imagine? Not for Penny.

Penny is a prostitute and a junkie. Penny also looks like a regular person, unthreatening, like someone you would send your kids to for lemonade and cookies. I met her on Third Street in Eureka on a chance encounter in the dark of night. She was wearing black jeans, a big overcoat, carrying a simple black purse and a few books in the cradle of her arms. I had a gut feeling that she was what I wanted for my interview, so I walked up to her timidly and introduced myself.

She was hesitant to converse with me, until I made eye contact with her and assured her that I was not wired and carried no cameras. She explained that she was "working" and invited me to her home the next day.

Home turned out to be a dilapidated apartment building like something straight out of a modern drug movie. The stained, dirty hallway was littered with trash. Sounds of blaring televisions and random yelling emitted from neighboring apartments, yet there was an eerie silence as I knocked on Penny's door.

Penny emerged from her neighbor's apartment to greet me. She worried out loud about the directions she had given me, as well as the safety of a girl like me coming to a place like this. She had been playing with the neighbor's daughter who knew her not as a prostitute or a junkie but as "Auntie Penny." As we walked into her apartment, I noticed how attractive she was with her flowing hair and bangle bracelets. A woman in her early 50s, she could easily have been anyone's aunt or grandmother.

Her place had cracks in the ceilings and walls. The slanting floor made her chairs roll toward the windows. Penny apologized for the apartment's condition. She said she pays $300 per month to live in this place.

She explained that she was coming down from a heroin high. She said had shot up at 7 a.m. and was not feeling so well coming down. She began to talk, at what seemed to be a mile a minute. Her eyes occasionally opened and shut very slowly, as if her eyeballs rolled back into her head searching for her thoughts.

I had so many questions. She had so much to release. With so many long-lost memories, where do we begin?

Penny (not her real name) was born in Massachusetts in 1946. She moved with her mom, dad and two sisters to Orange County when she was 10. They were an upper-class family, with a big ranch house and a pool.

Penny was an average student, involved in her high school drill team and other activities. Each child was given a car at age 16. From all sides, they seemed to be a typical American family.

Underneath, her father was a raging alcoholic. Penny's parents fought often. Sometimes Penny would come home to find blood on the walls and her father passed out on the floor. Penny would often help Dad into bed and then join her sisters in attending to Mom's bruises. Dad would usually wake up the next morning with no recollection of the beating he had given to Mom the night before. Then one day Dad decided to start beating Penny's sisters. He spared Penny from his rage.

"He never hit me," Penny recalls. "But I never provoked him."

Penny began to weep as she reflected on the memories of her early years. She spoke of her sister who died of a drug overdose at the age of 21. Her father had beaten her severely just three weeks before.

Her mother died of a brain aneurysm.

"The garage door fell on her head and Dad wouldn't let her go to the doctor."

The father died soon from cirrhosis of the liver.

The abuse had ended, but the learned cycle of abuse and tragedy had not yet had its run.

Penny graduated from high school at the age of 17 and entered college. She received an associate's degree in business from a community college in Fullerton. In her early 20s, Penny took a job with an oil company and got married. She later went to work for an advertising agency in Los Angeles.

After six years of marriage, Penny's husband revealed that he was a transvestite; he liked to dress in women's clothing. He would go out after work dressed as a woman and come home looking like any other man. A year after the revelation, the marriage ended.

"It was like a dream I couldn't wake up from," Penny recalls. "I loved him so much. How could I not see that? I was so protected from those things growing up."

Her ex-husband, Kenneth W. Sandusky, is now the vice president of a major candy corporation, Penny said. She doesn't know if he is fully "out" now.

Devastated, Penny quit her job and moved to Eureka. She went on what she called "general relief," or welfare. She began smoking pot and taking acid to hide from her pain and depression.

She pulled herself out of this bout and landed a job, ironically, in the criminal justice system. She met a man during this time, and they had a son together. Their relationship ended after six years, Penny said, because of his abusive nature and his use of speed. This man introduced her to heroin.

As for the son?

"He is a bright, nice, soft-spoken young man," Penny says. "We are close, but he is not aware of what I am doing."

Penny is living the life of a prostitute and drug addict.

She said she does 1.5 grams of heroin daily. It costs about $30 for a half-gram, $50 for a gram, but Penny can often get a half-gram at a discount from a girlfriend.

When she was introduced to heroin, she got hooked and couldn't keep a job, so fellow addicts introduced her to prostitution.

Penny says she doesn't perform sexual intercourse with her dates, only oral sex. She charges her clients $30, and she usually has three "dates" per night. She works as many as seven nights per week.

She describes her approach to work as cold and calculated.

"I just do my job, get my money and go home. I don't have to take my clothes off, and if they don't want to use a rubber then they have to leave."

She has regular customers, some of whom she recognizes from working in the criminal justice system. She also said that she has dated bank presidents, judges, lawyers and other "important men." Her dates are older men, many of whom are married.

"I have been very lucky," she said. "Younger men either want to rob you or rape you."

She chooses her clients with some care. On a typical night on the street, she looks for men driving nice cars and after getting in, she has the man drive her to a gas station. If she senses he is not an undercover agent and OK, they proceed to her apartment.

Penny says she has never been busted, but she has paid a price in other ways. Her constant shooting up led to the formation of abscesses on both hips. Heroin addicts who inject in the same place often form abscesses that won't heal. Botulism, a poisoning of the nerves, sets in. The abscesses have to be cut from the body. Penny has scars the size of fists on both hips. She has new abscesses growing on her legs.

Penny wants to get her life together so she can help herself and others. With her knowledge and history, she knows the pain and suffering that goes along with her lifestyle of prostitution and drug use. She hopes to save a few lives with that experience.

"None of us are proud of what we are doing," Penny says. "I'd like to go into a rehabilitation program, a year-long program maybe. I would like to work with young girls who are doing this with no protection."

On Sept. 30, a police sting in Old Town Eureka resulted in several arrests of suspected prostitutes and clients. This was the same night I met Penny, who was not one of the arrested.

A police official explained that women caught for prostitution are usually cited and released. A second citation could result in jail time, but it is a rare occurrence. There were 10 arrests and 10 convictions in 2001, according to criminal records.

Heroin addicts in Humboldt County can get help from detox centers and outpatient counseling services.

Somewhere, in any town, in any state, there are several women like Penny selling their bodies to survive. They may be heroin addicts or just trying to put food on the table for their children. They might be from a "normal" family or running from the abuse of a raging, alcoholic husband or father. They may be many things.

Nevertheless, they walk the darkened streets wearing little clothing or a big overcoat laden with books, bangle bracelets and a head full of vivid memories.

Respond briefly to the following.

1. What are the biggest legal or ethical problems this story presents?

2. What potential issues do you, as editor, face with this story?

3. What sorts of credibility issues do you see with this piece and how would you address them?

4. What case studies in journalism have you read about that are relevant to this situation?

5. Explain the relevance of the Janet Cooke/Washington Post case to this situation.

6. The police obtain a court order demanding that your newspaper surrender the name of the prostitute. If you refuse to do so, the reporter and possibly others on the editorial staff, including you, might be found in contempt of court and jailed. What do you do? Are you ready to go to jail to protect a source?

Other editing questions:

1. Comment on the reporter's use of the first person. What issues does it create?

2. How do you think the writer handles this potentially disturbing subject matter? Are there points where she is too explicit? How would you address that? How can you strike a balance between the writer's style of gritty realism and the concern for not upsetting or offending your readers?

3. Is there enough background in this story? Does it need more historical and cultural context about prostitution?

4. How do you handle Penny's claim that some of her clients include local judges, lawyers and businessmen? Do you need to have this verified somehow?

CHAPTER 7

Editing Information

Exercise I: Finding Story Ideas

Briefly respond to the following.

1. You are an assistant city editor given the task of generating local story ideas for your general assignment reporters. Make a list of 10 sources for possible ideas.

2. When trying to generate local story ideas, how can you use large national newspapers, magazines or the television networks?

3. Situation: You read in Time magazine that a new Nobel Prize winner lived in your town for four years and attended seventh through 10th grades there. How would you develop this? How would you determine its relevance?

4. Situation: You see on CNN that a naval officer arrested for treason is from your town, and his wife and children still live there. How would you develop this? How would you determine its relevance?

5. Situation: You see that USA Today has published a list of students who have won prestigious national scholarships. You notice one is from your local area. How would you develop this? How would you determine its relevance?

6. Situation: You see on a financial news network that the stock of a local high-tech company has plummeted more than 75 percent in one day. The president of the company is also a city councilman. How would you develop this? How would you determine its relevance?

7. Situation: You read in an education journal that your local university's philosophy department is in danger of losing its accreditation. How would you develop this? How would you determine its relevance?

8. Situation: You read in an international trade journal that a city in Korea is considering joining with your town in a "sister city" relationship. How would you develop this? How would you determine its relevance?

9. Generate a list of five local story ideas from information you find in national publications or television broadcasts.

Exercise II: Developing Story Ideas

1. You receive the following story memo from one of your cityside reporters. Write a response memo advising her on how to proceed.

Last Sunday the Rent Stabilization Board held its first poetry slam. The competition, according to the New York Times, was "believed to be the first competitive poetry performance sponsored by a city agency." Poets from the local area competed for cash prizes, as well as the right to publicly denounce their landlords and the spaces they rent. We didn't cover it. I want to find some local citizens who participated in this event and get their impressions of it. Also, I want to find some landlords who were "slammed" and get their reactions.

2. You receive this story memo from another cityside reporter. Write a response memo advising him how to proceed.

Earlier this month, the national papers ran stories about the U.S. Court of Appeals in our region voting to let the Pledge of Allegiance be voluntary in the public schools. I want to get local opinions on this issue. I plan to talk to teachers, principals, students and parents. I also want to speak to local church people about the "under God" clause in the pledge, which seems to be the flashpoint of the controversy.

3. Write a response memo for the following story pitch.

I want to do a local piece about affirmative action. The New York Times recently had a piece arguing that American debate over affirmative action in college admissions policies has grown increasingly civil in the last 10 years. This is in contrast to the early 1990s, when it was such a divisive, hot-button issue. The Times article states that many Americans have been quick to understand the entirety of affirmative action, and quick to grasp its most useful applications. I want to interview local college students to see what they think.

Exercise III: Sources and Credibility

Give short answers to the following questions.

1. Situation: You are the city editor. One of your reporters has written a story about air safety at your local airport. He has information revealing that there have been more than a dozen near-midair collisions in the past month, and the main reason is faulty old equipment used by the air traffic controllers. His sources are a leader of the controllers union and a spokesman for an independent air-safety watchdog group. They don't provide any documents to back up their claims, and the local spokesman for the Federal Aviation Administration refuses to comment. Do you have a story? Why or why not? How do you proceed?

2. Situation: You are the city editor. One of your general-assignment reporters has developed some information about racism in the local police department. Minority police officers are complaining that they are being passed over for promotions and treated unfairly in other ways. They say they are marshaling their forces for a racial-discrimination lawsuit, and have contacted a famous attorney for possible representation. You ask your longtime police-beat reporter for confirmation of this information, but he shrugs it off, saying that there's no discrimination in the police department. You know, in fact, that your beat reporter is close to the highest ranking officers in the department and has been successful over the years getting good stories because the police trust him. Would it be wrong to suspect that his judgment on this particular story might be compromised? If you do suspect this, how do you proceed?

3. Situation: You are the city editor. Your education reporter has discovered a shortfall of about $200,000 in the school district's budget for last year. The superintendent vehemently denies it, saying that your reporter's numbers are off. However, one of the members of the school board provides an independent accountant's report showing that about $200,000 is unaccounted for. It turns out that this school board member, who is known to be a bitter enemy of the superintendent, is the one who provided this information to your reporter. The other board members say there should be more investigation, but thus far are not willing to go on the record with their comments. How do you proceed?

4. Situation: A woman sends a letter to the editor saying her water tasted funny, so she hired some experts to test it. They found an unusually high lead content. She also claims she organized her neighbors to test their water, and they also found high lead. How would you approach this story?

5. Situation: A riot breaks out at a rap festival attended by 55,000 people. One of your reporters turns in a story about the scene inside the coliseum, describing in great detail some incidents involving assault, battery and use of firearms. There are also details about use of drugs by fans and assaults upon police by fans. You find out later that this reporter was not at the scene, but got all of her information from police sources. Another reporter, who actually was at the scene, contradicts the first reporter, telling you that it was the police who got out of control. This reporter claims the conflict was racial in nature because white police officers were provoked by the taunting of the mostly black and Latino crowd. You call a friend of yours because you know her children were at the concert. You speak with them on the phone. The children, who are white, tell you that the police were at fault. They tell you that everything was going well until the band onstage started doing an anti-police song and then "the cops just lost it and started beating heads." How do you determine the credibility of the sources? What interests could be affecting each subject's account of the situation?

6. Situation: One of your reporters who specializes in political affairs submits a story saying that the mayor is considering a possible run for governor. The story quotes unnamed sources within the mayor's inner circle, but includes no comment from the mayor himself. You know that the mayor is about to make a speech at a local convention, and you know you have a reporter covering that convention. You reach your reporter by cell phone and tell him to ask the mayor point-blank if he is running for governor. About an hour later, your reporter at the convention tells you that the mayor just laughed at the question and said he is definitely not running for governor. The mayor also adds: "I know you guys like to make things up sometimes, but this time you're really fishing." You confront the political reporter with this information and he flies into a rage, telling you he absolutely stands behind the story. He also says that he will complain to the publisher unless you run the story. What do you do? Why?

7. Situation: The reporter who covers the county courts tells you he has a story about a local judge who is taking bribes from certain high-powered attorneys to rule favorably on their cases. He doesn't have any documentation to back up this claim. He has it on background from the ex-wife of the judge, who is now married to an attorney. The attorney she's married to is a rival of the attorneys who have been winning cases by allegedly bribing the judge. What do you do with this information? Why?

Exercise IV: Online Tools/Using the Web

Respond briefly to the following.

1. Make a brief, rank-ordered list of what you think are the best search engines. Tell what unique features sets each apart from the others.

2. What search strategy would you use to get a prioritized list of Web sites about Saddam Hussein and his rise to power in Iraq?

3. What search strategy would you use to get a prioritized list of Web sites about President Richard Nixon's resignation in 1974?

4. What search strategy would you use to get information about Madonna's earnings over the last 10 years?

5. What Web sites are good for finding the authors of books? List at least five sites.

6. What Web sites are best for finding the correct spelling of someone's name? Let's use skater Tara Lipinski as an example. Many Web designers don't bother to check spellings. What Web sites would be considered perfectly legitimate sources for the correct spelling of Lipinski's name? List at least five.

7. Find two or three seemingly credible Web sites that misspell her name.

8. Try the same experiment with Britney Spears. How many hits do you get when you spell her name correctly? Try it again, this time misspelling her first name, either Brittany or Britany. How many hits do you get with those misspellings?

9. Find other celebrities whose names are routinely misspelled on carelessly made Web sites. List at least five.

10. List at least five Web sites you can trust for the correct spellings of names generally.

Exercise V: Vocabulary for Internet Use and Web Design

Write brief definitions for the following terms.

1. hyperlink
2. hypertext transfer protocol
3. home page
4. dot com
5. convergence
6. eyeballs
7. banners
8. code
9. webmaster
10. frames
11. Dreamweaver
12. keywords
13. Boolean
14. server
15. slide show
16. thumbnails
17. right click
18. download
19. bookmark
20. clipboard

21. browser
22. URL
23. absolute paths
24. WAV
25. MPEG
26. GIF
27. marquee
28. Pentium
29. domain
30. TCP/IP
31. shareware
32. Java
33. imagemap
34. newsgroup
35. dialog box
36. FAQ
37. applet
38. extensions
39. toolbar
40. signature

Exercise VI: Web Design

Respond briefly to the following.

Situation #1: You are the webmaster of your local newspaper. You've been assigned to design a site about city government information. What sorts of information would you put on the site? What links would you provide?

Situation #2: You've been asked to create a chat space for readers of your newspaper. What steps must you take to create this? What kinds of hardware and software must you have? How would users get access to the chat room? How would your newspaper monitor activity in this chat space?

CHAPTER 8
Editing Meaning: The Big Picture

Exercise I: Finding the Focus

CASE STUDY #1

You are the city editor of a major newspaper in Oakland, Calif. One of your reporters covering the local courts turns in the following story.

A lawyer for an Oakland junkyard owner needs more time to examine new evidence obtained yesterday that may prove her client innocent of the murder and assault charges brought against him.

Defense attorney Edward Coppin asked a district judge to postpone setting a trial date for William "Billy the Kid" Cummings during the defendant's brief appearance in Oakland-Alameda Municipal Court yesterday. Coppin said new physical evidence that may prove Cummings innocent has been obtained by Alameda County sheriff's deputies.

"Our position is looking better," Coppin said.

In addition, he said Cummings' neighbors have recently come forward with evidence to help the 51-year-old North Oakland resident. He is charged with the slaying of one Hayward man and the wounding of another with a pistol on May 21.

The shooting resulted in the death of 29-year-old Jamal Jennings and an assault on Jorge Oribado, 28, after they drove onto a lot on 7th Street where Cummings keeps about 80 deteriorating cars and trucks.

Cummings told police he tried to detain the alleged trespassers at gunpoint after spotting their blue Dodge Colt drive up the dirt road leading onto his property. He said they were going to vandalize one of his vehicles.

After a brief stop, however, Jennings was shot in the chest when he put the car in reverse and stepped on the gas to get away from the gunman, court records stated. He had no pulse and was not breathing when police arrived.

He was pronounced dead upon arrival at Highland Hospital in Oakland.

Oribado was shot in the right buttock as he ran from the car.

He apparently managed, however, to reach the front porch of a couple living close by. Greg and Noreen Quiros called 911 when they saw Oribado in a blood-stained shirt standing outside their front door, according to statements they made to deputies.

Oribado told the couple he and Jennings were "joyriding." He was hospitalized for several days.

Court records also stated that Jennings told his girlfriend earlier that day he was going to a junkyard in Oakland to look for a tire for their car.

Over the past year, Cummings said he had been experiencing problems with people vandalizing his property and stealing from his vehicles.

Coppin said there is a possibility Jenkins and Oribado trespassed on Cummings' lot more than once.

"I'm hoping that we can prove they were on the property several times," the lawyer said.

Deputy District Attorney Jim Caroompas said no prosecutor has been assigned to the case.

Provide some short answers to the following.

1. What are the problems with this story?

2. What absolutely must be fixed or eliminated?

3. How would you evaluate the lead?

4. The lead speaks of some "new evidence" cited by the defense attorney. Is this properly developed in the story?

5. Is there any information that is not in here that should be? What do you suggest the writer follow up on?

6. Are there any inconsistencies in the story?

7. Did you find any sentences that were confusing to the reader? How would you improve them?

8. How would you speak to the writer about the problems in this story? What would you have the writer do to make the story better?

9. What if the writer is not available and there are two hours to go before deadline? What can you do to try to develop this story? If nothing can be done to this story by deadline, what should you do?

Exercise II: Fixing Unfocused Stories

CASE STUDY #2

You are the features editor of a major newspaper. One of your reporters turns in the following local feature story. Your reporter has been given permission to write this story in the first person.

Two flags greet visitors at the entrance to the brightest house on the block. Inside they'd find themselves face-to-face with an amazing man.

His name is Alvin Knopfler, also known as our town's "Patriotic Legend." His 21-year military career includes serving in the Navy during World War II and in the Army during the Korean conflict.

As a member of Company A, the 14th engineer combat battalion in Korea, Knopfler applied his skills and courage to the demolition of bridges, the laying and clearing of mine fields, the building and repairing of roads and bridges, and serving on the front line as an infantryman.

Knopfler has been a member of the local chapter of the Veterans of Foreign Wars for 45 years.

Knopfler eagerly invites visitors around to the side of his house to view his incredible back yard. The landscape is impeccable, with hedges perfectly hand-trimmed in a plethora of shapes. He loves to point out his favorites: the liberty bell ivy that surrounds the cherry tree he once cut down, the evening star and the heart of ivy that is next to the front door. The legacy of Betsy Ross' creation waves all about the yard. Some flap in neat rows. Others are lone flyers. A wooden Uncle Sam stands proud.

Knopfler and his wife, Paula, live in the same house where he was born in September 1923.

The local newspaper profiled Knopfler on his birthday. They dubbed him "The Patriotic Legend."

"When I'm out here, I am closer to the folks. It is kind of sentimental," Knopfler said, his blue eyes welling up with tears. "My dad is here, and my mom is here. Dad was strict, but was good looking, honest and had a lot of pride. He would always be there for you. Lots of memories are out here."

The Knopfler home is a museum within a museum. Patriotic mementos and artifacts surround the interior. There are photos of presidents and many war medals. Lincoln, Truman and Eisenhower calmly gaze from their framed homes on the walls. Collected Statues of Liberty stand tall about the room. Lady Liberty holds her torch high amidst the stars and stripes of one displayed flag.

There are hundreds of items representative of the history of the United States, and Knopfler said it was impossible to choose which is his favorite. He did point to a huge picture of two flags crossing. One flag had 13 stars on it, and the other had 48.

"Our forefathers worked so hard to put things together," he said.

One of Knopfler's concerns is that people don't know enough about the country's history and that they don't have an appreciation of all the lives that have been lost and the hundreds of thousands of men and women who fought for our freedom. He said he wishes people would care more about each other and for those who have fought so hard. Even through all that he has seen and experienced, however, he still has a bright outlook on life.

"You have to look at people—they aren't all that bad," Knopfler said. "Everyone has a little good in their heart. I love what I do and what life is all about. We all need help some time or another. I like helping other people. You don't close the door on anybody. Many people in the world today need help. We are fortunate that we live in such a wonderful country."

Knopfler then touched on what is currently happening in the world, which makes him saddened and hurt. There was pain in his eyes.

"It's tough, very tough. Sometimes when I am walking, I feel so hurt inside. I get to where I feel so hurt I am crying. The last couple of times my wife saw my tears come down, but I tell her I hurt more inside than the tears can show. I look at life a little different than a lot of people. And if you feel it inside, you will show it," he said.

Although it is apparent that Knopfler hurts for the world around him, there seemed to be much love and happiness between him and his wife. They are kind and gracious to visitors. Paula gave this reporter a bag filled with small flags, along with several big hugs.

We have a hero living among us who has been forgotten by most. Alvin Knopfler is one of those guys you see every day, but don't take the time to know. He walks everywhere and enjoys spending time downtown inquiring about the lives of others. You will know him when you see him, as he often wears a baseball cap that reads, "Alvin, the Patriotic Legend."

Respond briefly to the following.

1. What is the point of this story? Summarize it in one or two sentences.

2. Write some alternate leads that bring better focus to the story.

3. Is there a timeliness element that can be brought to this story? Is there a novelty element?

4. Does this story have enough information? What questions do you want the reporter to answer that she doesn't?

5. The reporter refers to her subject as an "amazing man." Did the reporter make this case convincingly in this story?

6. Evaluate the tone of the reporter. Do you think it is appropriate?

7. Think of some other ways this story could be focused. What suggestions would you give to the writer on focusing the story?

8. Are there parts where the writer needs to clarify either what Knopfler is saying or what she has written? What sections need to be developed further?

Exercise III: Improving the Lead and Finding the Focus

CASE STUDY #3

You are an assistant city editor. The city editor asks you to edit/rewrite this story.

SAN JOSE, Calif.—Why are the children of Eduardo W. Berroa still suing the estate of Francois Carpentier when there now appears to be a $50 million settlement?

There is no ready answer arising from the mysterious January 2001 murder of Carpentier, a multimillionaire high-tech entrepreneur, and his wife in Fremont.

It might be because the answer is hidden beneath mountains of depositions, affidavits and secret testimony before a grand jury. Giving sworn statements last week were Berroa's children, Jorge, 18, and Nonie, 19, who are suing the estate.

Appearing before the Alameda County grand jury was Carpentier's son, Joaquin, who is helping prosecutors in their murder case against Berroa's cousin, Emil Garcia.

Garcia, a former railroad worker, has eluded authorities and is believed to be hiding in Nebraska.

The Berroa lawsuit is set for trial in two weeks. Representing Carpentier's estate is attorney George Millican of Alameda.

Millican acknowledged that he and the attorneys for the plaintiffs reached a $50 million settlement, resolving a 10-year dispute about intellectual property rights involving computer software they had created together.

The plaintiffs, however, have not yet formally dropped the lawsuit.

"We're waiting until all the T's are crossed and all the I's are dotted," said Jorge Berroa.

Task #1: Try rewriting the story, using your best judgment.
Task #2: Try writing a few alternate leads that address different parts of the story.
Task #3: Respond briefly to the following.

1. What other information do you need to properly develop and rewrite this story?

2. If this is all the information you have, can you fashion a legitimate story out of this, or would it be better to hold it for more development the next day?

CASE STUDY #4

Situation: You are the special projects editor for a daily newspaper in a large, diverse city. You are putting together a package on "the immigrant experience." You assign one of your best writers to do a feature profile on a Chinese restaurant worker. He brings back this story.

There are thousands of them. They are invisible, or nearly so. You may have seen them out of the corner of your eye, picking up a life on the periphery. They work in steamy, tight kitchens, sliding fatty cuts of beef around or clearing dirty dishes. They clamp their mouths shut as the high-pressure sprayers work to evacuate the mustard or rice from chipped plates.

Robert Lee makes $800 a month, receives no health benefits and works more than 50 hours a week. This is the hard reality of many immigrants. Still, most would assert that the lifestyle is better here than in their homeland.

According to Lee, he has more opportunity here. He said one can have nothing and become something in the United States. Without friends or connections, in China you have almost no hope.

"You have to know people in China in order to become somebody there," Lee said. "Here it is different. If you work hard, you can succeed."

Lee has been accepted to San Francisco State University, where the fees are high for international students. He takes classes at a local community college because it costs less for the same classes. He needs more than $16,000 to attend San Francisco State for one semester, according to his projections. So Lee is studying at the community college and earning money working in a Chinese restaurant to cover his future semesters at the four-year university. He leaves his home in the Sunset District for school at 7:30 a.m. and goes from there to work at 3 p.m. His day isn't over until about midnight.

It is illegal for Lee to work while here on a student visa, but it is a necessary risk for him because it allows him to continue his education.

"Robert is very smart," said Mrs. Chen, the owner of the restaurant where Lee works. "He learn everything very fast. Now he cooks for us."

Despite the struggles of school and work, Lee has found his coming to America to be a life-changing experience: "My family is poor, so we couldn't travel. We stay in one place. China is very different from America."

Only about 20 percent of eligible students from China are selected to study abroad, Lee explained. They must be approved via an interview process with the U.S. Embassy. He only spoke Mandarin at his first interview, and he believes that was the reason he failed. The embassy interviewers watch for Chinese trying to pass themselves off as motivated students. The next time, he made an effort to speak English and he believes that was why his visa was approved.

Last year, nearly 40,000 visas were approved by U.S. immigration authorities. From that, nearly 13,000 came to California. A portion of these are students, professionals and relatives of U.S. citizens. Of course, these numbers don't account for illegal immigrants, who are often brought by a shadowy collection of outlaws known as "Snakeheads," akin to the "Coyotes" who traffic people from Mexico. The illegal route is expensive and dangerous, and the immigrants are often abused.

Today there are as many as 150 million living in poverty in China. A couple of years ago the average wage in the city was the equivalent of $700 a year, and in rural areas it was just over $200. It is no wonder that these Chinese poor hunger for the greater opportunities in the West.

Lee knows his chances of staying here legally are slim. None of his relatives are U.S. citizens. Without sponsorship, he will have to get a U.S. company to petition for his absolute necessity. Meanwhile, he is enjoying the comforts of American life.

He drives a platinum-colored 1991 Honda Prelude. His favorite American food is pizza. His favorite drink is Coca-Cola. He likes to watch the Mexican television station.

"I like America because there are so many kinds of people, so many religions and cultures," Lee said.

Although he loves most of the things he experiences here, Lee is critical of America's foreign interventions. "America needs to stop being the police of the world," he said flatly.

If Lee is lucky, he can save enough money for next fall's tuition and will not have to continue at the community college. His post-graduation plans include a return to China, where his new English skills will help him find a good job. Unless, of course, he can find a job here.

In the meantime, he will phone and write to his parents each week, send pictures twice a month, and e-mail his friends at the university in China regularly.

Today, Lee will smile and head back to the periphery, chasing relentlessly after the dream.

Respond briefly to the following.

1. What kind of lead did the writer use? Is it appropriate for this story? Is the lead material supported by subsequent information? Write an alternate lead.

2. Is there enough cultural information and statistics in the story to provide adequate background? What information is this story missing? Make a list of things you need to verify.

3. If you do decide to check the facts, where do you go to get them? Where do you get the immigration data? Where do you get the Chinese population and wages data? Where do you get the data about international-student tuition at San Francisco State?

4. Is the story organized well? Identify the narrative elements included.

5. How would you re-structure the story so that all the narrative elements flow?

6. In the story Lee admits that he is in the United States on a student visa and that he is working illegally. He asks the reporter not to use his real name because he fears deportation. Should we use a different name or his real name? Should we reveal the illegality of his work situation or not? Why?

7. What effect would using a false name have on the story? Should you take out the fact that he is working illegally?

8. What ethical and legal issues arise from reporting or not reporting that he is working illegally?

9. What if the federal immigration authorities call and demand that you give them the name of the student and the restaurant? Would you comply? Why or why not?

10. After the story is published, a local Chinese American community leader calls and complains that the story perpetuates bad stereotypes about Chinese being outlaws and menial laborers. How do you respond?

11. Evaluate the overall tone of the piece. Was it appropriate?

CASE STUDY #5

Read this story and answer the questions that follow.

The fear of terrorism still haunts the American psyche. Many believe the next great attack will come from foreign interests; others say we should not discount the possibility of domestic terror.

But which groups are likely to target us? Could it be members of such organizations as the Christian Identity, the Ku Klux Klan, the Aryan Nation or some other extreme faction? And then there is a segment of "terrorists" referred to as "eco-terrorists."

The group Earth First! has been labeled by some as "eco-terrorists." This is nothing new to Earth First! members, and they vehemently reject such a description.

"Earth First! is an anti-terrorist group," said Darryl Cherney, an Earth First! activist based in Northern California. "We believe in combating terrorists in order to protect all of Earth's creatures, including man, and we condemn acts of terrorism."

Cherney and Earth First! activist Judi Bari were actually the target of terrorist activity when a car bomb exploded with them in the car on May 24, 1990. Bari sustained crippling injuries and Cherney was also hurt. Bari died in 1997 of cancer. The bombing case is still unsolved, even though there is new DNA evidence. Cherney has been active with Earth First! for more than 15 years and finds the term "eco-terrorist," as used by law enforcement, to be very loaded.

North American researcher Barry Clausen articulates this concept of eco-terrorism. "If environmental terrorists had not emerged, terrorism in America would have been virtually non-existent in the late 1980s. It was during the 1980s that issues concerning the environment led some radical environmental communities to turn to terrorism."

When Earth First! began in 1980, its mission was to use a direct-action approach to protecting the Earth. Its Web site professes: "We believe in using all the tools in the tool box, ranging from grassroots organizing and involvement in the legal process to civil disobedience and monkey wrenching." The term "monkey wrenching" was popularized in the infamous novel by Edward Abbey, "The Monkey Wrench Gang," written in 1975.

A man of the wilderness, Abbey is considered by many to have fathered and fostered aspects of the environmental-activist movements through his cynical and often subversive books. He wrote unabashedly, speaking to what he saw as the willful destruction by corporate entities that threatened wilderness. Abbey's characters would engage in acts ranging from lighting billboards on fire to trashing tractors at job sites. Many "monkey wrenching" techniques were espoused for activist consumption in this landmark book that screamed vehemently at the reader for the need to preserve wild places, and this view has certainly been championed to large effect by Earth First!

Although the Earth First! mission remains the same, many of their approaches are different. Earth First! has been involved in several controversial acts since the early 1980s. Most of the actions were aimed at large corporations such as the timber industry, mining and ranching facilities. Cherney called such activities "sabotage," not terrorism.

These activists frustrate investigators by hitting remote targets, often at night, and leaving little evidence, but charred ruins. Earth First! is by no means the only group considered to be "eco-terrorists" by law enforcement agencies such as the FBI. One recent attack that received wide-ranging media attention took place in 1998 in Vail, Colorado. After the building of a ski-lift operation was complete, members of Earth First! said that the development was encroaching on a habitat for lynx. To make a direct point, a series of fires were lit around the perimeter of the ski lifts. More than $12 million in damage was done.

According to Cherney, Earth First! was never accused, on any level, of setting the fire. Members of the Earth Liberation Front claimed responsibility for the setting of the fires. But, since Earth First! was there "doing above-ground activist work," they got linked to the destruction.

These types of actions have some Earth Firsters proud and some others confused. The group is autonomous and does not have members, but activists. They also do not have organizational bylaws or hierarchy. So how do they view "eco-terrorism"?

One writer of the Earth First! Journal in Oregon, Rodney Coronado, disagrees with the term "eco-terrorism." He said the term was thought up by corporations and applied to a variety of small-time pranks, such as tree-sits, to prevent logging, or throwing animal entrails on public officials to protest hunting.

"I personally consider myself an anti-terrorist, because everything I oppose I see as acts of terrorism," Coronado said. "When I think of eco-terrorist, I think of corporate executive officers in high-rise buildings."

The official Web site suggests that the battle for conservation is not merely for keeping outdoor-recreation opportunities, or even for wise management and use of natural resources, but rather a fight for life itself, a fight for the survival of Earth. The Web site explains that we are losing animal species every day due to human expansion, and as a lack of serious care for the environment.

There are various ways to get a point across. Although some environmental activists believe in extreme action, like bombing an animal-testing site or making threatening phone calls to high-level corporate timber officials, this is not the belief of all environmentalists.

Julia "Butterfly" Hill offers this perspective on the role of violence in protest movements: "If this is the voice for forests, it's no wonder we're losing them."

Write brief answers to the following questions.

1. What kind of lead did the writer use? Is it appropriate for this story? Is the lead material supported by subsequent information? Write an alternate lead.

2. Is there enough cultural information and statistics in the story to provide adequate background? Make a list of the things you need to verify.

3. If you do decide to check the facts, where do you go to get them?

4. Is the story organized well? Identify the narrative elements included, and identify which are missing.

5. How would you re-structure the story so that all the narrative elements flow?

6. Does the author show a bias? To whom?

7. Are all sides of the story properly represented?

8. As the editor on this story, what would you do next?

CHAPTER 9

Working with Writers

Exercise I: Keeping an Open Mind

Situation: You are the city editor. You send a reporter to the local zoo to see if there is any substance to rumors you've heard about animal-care conditions there. She comes back with the following story.

Behind the redwood curtain on California's North Coast sits the state's oldest zoo, the city of Eureka's Sequoia Park Zoo. In its friendly confines lives Bill, the oldest male chimpanzee in captivity, and the third oldest in the world.

Bill has lived at the zoo for more than 45 years. He is currently the only chimp there.

Gretchen Ziegler, the zoo curator, said, "On the surface of things, when you first walk into the zoo, you see Bill in a situation that is not appropriate for chimpanzees. Most people realize that chimps are very social, and he is alone. The exhibit itself is small, outdated and not natural at all, and that is not very appropriate in this day and age. So you start to think, 'My gosh, this must be a really depressed, emotionally stressed animal,' but he is actually the most well-adjusted chimp I have ever seen or worked with. Typically in captivity, with primates like chimpanzees, you often will see stereotypical behaviors like pacing or twirling things that make you think, 'Oh, this isn't a psychologically healthy animal,' but Bill shows almost no stereotypical behaviors."

In 1957, a traveling circus came through the city of Eureka with 10-year-old Bill. Children from Washington School next door and local residents raised $500 from community donations and purchased Bill from the circus, for the zoo. According to Court Matthews, the Sequoia Parks zookeeper, the traveling circus saw Bill as a liability.

When chimpanzees reach sexual maturity (10 years old or so), they are no longer manageable, and are dangerous, he said. Bill appeared before crowds in London, New York and in the world-famed Moulin Rouge. He was also a star on "The Ed Sullivan Show."

Ziegler said animals, especially primates, have their own personalities. Chimpanzees, especially males, tend to be pretty excitable. It's not to say you can't develop a rapport with gorillas, chimps and orangutans and be somewhat safe. But with an adult male, the chances of you being safe are quite a bit less than young animals. For this reason there is no direct human contact with Bill, and zookeepers do not enter his primary habitat.

For many years he had a neighbor named Ziggy, another male chimp. Ziggy and Bill shared a habitat with a wall separating the two. Ziggy died in 1996, and the wall separating the two enclosures was removed, giving Bill more space.

Although at 57 years old Bill is now considered a dangerous primate, in a sense Bill has never really been a chimp, Ziegler said. He was hand-raised by humans. In a circus environment you treat chimps like humans, and he has never been in a normal chimp social situation, so he sees himself as one of us.

Respond briefly to the following:

1. Evaluate how the reporter responded to the assignment. Make a list of issues you have with this story.

2. As city editor, are you still interested in this story? Why or why not?

3. Can the information be delivered in a different way? Is historical information and quote material used properly?

4. How would you work with the writer on this story? How would you advise her on how to proceed?

Situation: You are the entertainment editor for a major newspaper. One of your staff rock critics turns in this negative review of a new Eric Clapton recording.

If Eric Clapton's best music is like fine wine, then buying a new Clapton CD is like uncorking an unfamiliar Cabernet. You just don't know what you're going to get.

If you're very lucky, you'll get vintage Clapton. You'll get a set of blistering blues rockers with dazzling solos from the hand of God himself, as in 1994's "From the Cradle."

If you're not so lucky, you'll get something pretentious and unrealized. You'll get Clapton trying on different styles and sounding quite flawed, sounding not quite there, like in too many other albums he's recorded in the past decade or so.

Unfortunately, the latter is the case with Clapton's latest offering, "Reptile," which reached Humboldt County stores this week.

"Reptile" features a handful of blues-flavored cover tunes, ranging from James Taylor's "Don't Let Me Be Lonely Tonight," to Ray Charles' "Come Back Baby," as well as five original songs. The tracks were recorded last summer in Los Angeles and feature guest appearances by Texas bluesman Doyle Bramhall, keyboardist Billy Preston and R&B vocalists the Impressions.

There was a good deal of anticipation for "Reptile" because fans wanted to see how Clapton would follow the huge success of last year's "Riding With the King," the collaborative recording with B.B. King, which has sold more than 1.7 million CDs and tapes so far worldwide.

Fans appreciated Clapton's leisure cruise with B.B., but were not entirely satisfied with his understated playing on that album. They hunger for the volcanic Clapton of "Did You Ever Love a Woman" and "White Room" and "Crossroads" and any number of masterworks from his distant past. Those who thirst for the Clapton of old, however, will only get a taste on

"Reptile." Most of the album sounds like some homogenized crossover attempts and leftover stuff from his lesser albums of the last 20 years.

"Reptile" (the opening track) and "Believe in Life" sound like something straight out of the George Benson school of boring, fern-bar jazz. "Got You on My Mind," with its boozy ambience and bluesy chorus, sounds like something from his ill-informed Delaney and Bonnie catalog. "Superman Inside" would fit quite nicely in any of Clapton's undistinguished albums of the 1980s.

"Traveling Light" has a nice dark groove, but it sounds unoriginal, like a combination of "After Midnight" and "Cocaine." No surprise really, especially since it was written by J.J. Cale, who also wrote those two other songs.

There is some bright light in this fog, though.

"I Ain't Gonna Stand For It," a call-and-response rocker penned by Stevie Wonder, has a cool, defiant tone and lights a fire underneath Clapton, who tosses in some nice riffing. "Broken Down" has some tasty acoustic work.

Far and away the guitar highlight of the album, though, is the break on "Come Back Baby," which hints at some of the passion from "Layla"—the electric version, not the unplugged version—and echoes the blazing glory of "From the Cradle."

This lead break lasts just 45 seconds, but it alone is worth the price of the CD. It is Clapton roaring, flinging lightning bolts, flying, gliding, testifying, hesitating, teasing, moaning and finally finding salvation in his sorrow.

Nobody bends a note to its perfect place and sets it alight quite like Clapton does. No one hops around the blues scale and the harmonic minors with such articulation and clarity. No one embodies more the legacy of electric blues.

Any new Clapton release will be an event, no matter how good or mediocre the music. They remind us of the glory that was Eric Clapton. They remind us of the magical Cream years, the Derek & the Dominoes masterworks, the possibilities fully realized in "Slowhand."

A coterie of new fans discovered Clapton in recent years when he scored big hits with his softer material, "Tears in Heaven" and the tunes from "Unplugged." Those of us who've followed his work for many years knew he had a soft side, a side we heard in the 1970s in the achingly beautiful "Thorn Tree in the Garden" from the "Layla" double album.

So we laughed off this "discovery" of the new Clapton, as sensitive singer-songwriter churning out soft hits. We've always known that deep inside there is a full-bodied, mellowed, digestible Cabernet that would complement any civilized dinner.

We just want to hear him throw some lightning one more time.

Respond briefly to the following.

1. What is your reaction to this review?

2. How would you evaluate the lead and the structure of this review?

3. Does the review contain any inaccurate information? If so, what? How would you check the information?

4. Is there libel in the review? If so, what are the libelous statements?

5. How would you coach the reviewer to make this piece better?

Exercise II: Improving Stories

Situation: You send a reporter out to write a story about the state of women's athletics at the local university. She turns in this piece.

Oct. 15 was the first official day for Laurie Murphy and her basketball teammates to start their practices for the upcoming season. But before Murphy's basketball practice at 3 p.m., she had a full day ahead of her. Murphy has a 9 a.m. beginning reporting class. She has to make sure to leave her house early enough to find parking, which takes her at least 30 minutes. At 10 a.m., she has a communications and law class that takes about an hour. When 11 a.m. hits and she has a two-hour break, she uses this time to do homework or simply take a nap if she is exhausted from the day before.

By 2 p.m., Murphy has a public relations class to attend. This class will take another hour out of her day. When 3 p.m. finally arrives, it is time for basketball practice. Today Murphy and teammates shot baskets for 15 minutes, ran sprints, worked on their free throws and offensive and defensive drills. Then they had a 15-minute scrimmage before having to make 20 free throws at the end.

This is an average day for student-athletes at the university. They have the burden of being both students and athletes. "Students don't realize we have to work harder," says Nenita Herrera, a 100- and 400-meter hurdler on the university track team. "We have to do schoolwork just like everyone else and still be able to play our sport."

An average day for today's female athletes is somewhat symbolic of the struggle women had 30 years ago, when they fought to have the same rights men do to play sports. Title IX, which enabled women to be able to play sports in educational institutions, was signed by President Richard Nixon in 1972, under the Educational Amendments of 1972 to the Civil Rights Act of 1964. It states that no one can be excluded on the basis of gender from participation in "any educational program or activity receiving federal assistance."

This law was created to prevent sex discrimination against women students, as well as women employees of educational institutions. These days, Title IX has brought intercollegiate athletics into sharp focus.

The university finances 12 intercollegiate athletics programs. These programs are divided into seven sport programs for women and five sport programs for men. The programs, which were reviewed recently for adherence to federal guidelines, are required to abide by Title IX regulations.

The university has undertaken a number of projects and is considering several proposals to bring greater gender equity into its athletic programs. For example, the university is presently working with the State Department of Boating and Waterways to construct a boat instruction and safety center for the women's rowing program. The center will have a boat bay, training room, locker room area and equipment room.

Other proposals are the remodeling of the women's locker room facilities and the construction of an off-campus softball field. Olivia Oyler, a softball assistant coach, has noticed the changes university athletics have made: "I have seen big changes in the last couple of years. Administrators are taking time to focus on female athletes with the new locker room, new softball field, and new rowing house for the crew team. They are making equal opportunities for female athletes."

To benefit female athletes and to enhance the women's intercollegiate programs, two additional staff positions were added: Assistant Sports Information Director Georgette O'Connor and Coach Oyler. Some believe more hires could be made.

Despite these advances, the university still has its share of critics. "I don't think administration has been doing a good job in bringing in more coaches," says Christine Nako, a rugby forward. "They need to bring in better coaches for both male and female programs."

Another significant component of Title IX is the allocation of supplementary athletic program elements. Equal treatment is supposed to be provided in coaching, travel per diem allowances, medical and training facilities, equipment and supplies, recruitment of student athletes, and publicity.

One player feels comfortable with the expenses given to the team she plays for. Joyce Perey, center mid-fielder on the women's soccer team, says, "We have it up on the football team because there are less of us and we can eat whatever we want. Since there are more of them, they are limited to where they can eat. "

All in all, intercollegiate athletics at the university have worked to improve and demonstrate a positive and equitable environment for female athletes, many believe. Coach Oyler reflected back to how she was treated when she was an undergraduate playing softball. "I was treated great. We got a lot of support from the staff and community."

Oyler attended a Division I school before coming to the university and she did not get the same recognition. She felt she was just considered a number.

"At this school you get more personal attention from the staff. This place is more family-oriented and you get more camaraderie from this community."

"The athletes as a whole are a close-knit group," Perey said. "The athletic programs have made a positive impact. All the teams support one another."

Respond briefly to the following.

1. Is this story ready to run? Why or why not?

2. What else does this story need?

3. What works in this story and what doesn't?

4. How would you advise the reporter on how to make the story better? Make a script for how you would talk to the writer.

5. Do you see any potential for sidebars? If so, write a proposal for one.

CHAPTER 10

Writing Headlines

Exercise I: Headline Vocabulary

Write brief descriptions for the following.

1. Hammer

2. Slammer

3. Downstyle

4. Flush left

5. Deck

6. Banner

7. Skyline banner

8. Ragged right

9. Leading

10. Woodenhed

11. Tombstones

12. Dummy

13. Kicker

14. Overline

15. Flag

16. Kerning

17. HTK

Exercise II: Counting Headlines

1. You are the copy desk chief. You assign one of your copy editors a headline to write; two lines, with a count of 26 per line. Wiggle room is 3 counts under or 1 1/2 counts over. The copy editor turns in the headline below. Does it fit the count?

   Ethical research issues take
   center stage in Kansas City

2. You assign a headline of one line, with a count of 21. Wiggle room is the same as above. Does the following headline fit the count?

   Death row inmate freed

3. You assign a headline of two lines, with a count of 19 per line. Wiggle room is the same as above. Does the following headline fit the count?

   FAA issues new rules
   for checked-in baggage

Exercise III: Writing Headlines

Edit the following stories and write headlines for them. Wiggle room for headlines is 3 under and 1 1/2 over.

COUNT: One line of 33, down style, flush left.

EUREKA, Calif.—State Sen. Wesley Chesbro on Monday officially announced that he is a candidate for re-election.

The Democrat turned in 3,000 signatures from 2nd Senate District voters at the office of the Humboldt Country registrar of voters. He presented the nomination petition at registrars' offices in Lake, Mendocino, Napa and Sonoma counties later in the day.

The only Republican to file candidacy for the seat so far is Peggy Redfearn, who owns and operates a cleaning service in Lake County. Chesbro has no opponent in the Democratic primary.

COUNT: Main head: three lines of 12, down style, flush left. Deck head: two lines of 31, down style, flush left.

PORTLAND, Ore.—Salmon on both sides of the Pacific Rim need protection more than ever as scientists learn more about their diversity and their effect on other species, even trees, top fisheries experts said Monday.

Dan Bottom of the National Marine Fisheries Service opened a two-day conference of experts from four countries warning the Pacific Northwest is "experiencing an aquatic biodiversity crisis."

Bottom said more than 200 salmon stocks are at risk of extinction or threatened, a decline that roughly follows the level of development along the Pacific Rim. In more populated and industrialized areas, the fish decline is more apparent than in remote areas.

"The picture is not pretty," he said.

COUNT: One line of 18, down style, flush left.

AKRON, Ohio—"Tiger" Woods won his third consecutive NEC Invitational championship with a dramatic victory over Jim Fuyrk on the 7th hole at Firestone Country Club here.

Both men finished the first 72 holes with a 12-under-par total of 268. Woods shot rounds of 66, 67, 67 and 69 while Furyk had scores of 65, 66, 66 and 71.

"It was a war," Woods said. "Neither one of us gave an inch. It was fun to complete like that, where you were tested to the absolute utmost." Furyk said, "I don't feel like I let anyone down today. I played well enough to win." I thought I won the tournament a couple of times today.

In the playoff, Woods sank a 2 foot birdey putt and then raised both arms over his shoulders like a heavy-weight boxing champion. "That's the ultimate. Win or lose, to be out there in that enviroment is pretty cool."

Tiger now has a playoff record of 7-1. He received one million dollars for his victory and now has earned more than $25 million in a career that began just 6 years ago.

COUNT: One line of 57. Use down style, flush left.

BERKELEY, Calif.—Cleanup work on Telegraph Avenue should be finished today, more than 20 weeks after fire destroyed three buildings near Sproul Plaza.

"It's mostly just a matter of sweeping up now," building contractor James Jensen said Thursday evening. "We'll do some final testing this week."

Berkeley officials said the city hopes to reopen Ninth Street early next week, possibly by Monday.

Although the work started later than expected, the contractor said, it was completed at less than the estimated cost.

"It's been a most interesting, very difficult job," Jensen said. "There were three different owners and about seven regulatory agencies involved. But after some kicking and scratching, everybody agreed on a re-building plan."

Jensen's firm, Jensen & Meyers Construction, was hired in July to clear away the debris of the three buildings—a tobacco shop, a shoe store and a book store—but was not able to start work until the end of that month.

Exercise IV: Problem Headlines

You are the news editor, with the power to accept or reject headlines submitted by the copy desk. Tell why the following headlines are or are not acceptable. If you reject a headline, write an alternate one using approximately the same count.

1. For a story about Jerry Brown considering another run for president, this headline is submitted:

   Brown eyes another
   run at Oval Office

2. For a story about a senior-citizen golf tournament, this headline is turned in:

   Senior tournament adds
   new wrinkle to golf scene

3. A murder suspect, accused of committing a series of grisly murders, is killed in prison. This headline is turned in:

   Justice comes early
   for accused serial killer

4. Roseanne Arnold parodies the national anthem at the opening ceremonies of a major league baseball game and is roundly booed by fans. This headline is turned in:

   It's over: the Fat Lady sings

5. Two tornadoes ravage Lawrence, Kansas. Police say the death toll might reach more than 100. This headline is turned in:

   The night of the twisters;
   police fear many dead

6. A city in Delaware considers a ban on cigarette smoking in public places. This headline is turned in:

   Your right to light
   goes up in smoke

7. Emmitt Smith of the Dallas Cowboys surpasses a career yardage record after a long, grueling chase. This headline is turned in:

   It's official: Emmitt rules!

8. A group of armed robbers bursts into a restaurant and takes money from customers and the cash register. This headline is turned in:

   Robbery interferes with eating

9. For a travel story about the author's search for her roots in Guam, this headline is submitted:

   A cultural connection

10. During an insurance-fraud trial, the prosecutor tells the jury that the defendant forged a son's signature. This headline is submitted:

    Husband forged
    son's signature
    for insurance

11. For a story about an association of prostitutes asking the mayor to liberalize local sex-for-hire laws, this headline is submitted:

    Prostitutes appeal to mayor

12. For a story about an axe murder, this headline is submitted:

    After vicious axe murder,
    family tries to pick up pieces

CHAPTER 11

Thinking Visually

Exercise I: Photo Editing Vocabulary

Write brief definitions for the following.

1. Proportion wheel

2. Silhouette

3. Line shot

4. Halftone

5. The "dime rule"

Exercise II: Digital Photography Vocabulary

Write brief definitions for the following.

1. Thumbnail

2. JPEG

3. TIFF

4. DPI

5. Megapixels

Exercise III: Graphics/Illustrating Statistics

How would you illustrate this passage from a story about local minority voting trends?

Locally, minorities heavily favored Democrats in the past 10 presidential elections. In the 2000 election, 62 percent of the minority vote went to Al Gore. In his two victories, Bill Clinton received 71 percent (1992) and 73 percent (1996).

Michael Dukakis got 53 percent of the local minority vote in 1988, despite finishing a distant second to George Bush in the national popular vote. Local minorities also voted decisively Democratic in 1984 (Walter Mondale, 58 percent), 1980 (Jimmy Carter, 60 percent), 1976 (Carter, 59 percent), 1972 (George McGovern, 57 percent), 1968 (Hubert Humphrey, 56 percent) and 1964 (Lyndon Johnson, 61 percent).

Exercise IV: Using Graphics

Respond briefly to the following.

1. Describe a situation when it would be appropriate to pull material out of a story and create a separate story or sidebar.

2. What is the difference between a bar graph, a line chart and a pie chart? Describe the most appropriate ways to use each.

3. What is the most popular infographic? Why?

4. What is shown with an exploded-view diagram? Describe an instance when it could be used. Find an example in a recent newspaper.

5. What is the difference between a credit line and a source line?

6. What is the difference between a cutline and a slug?

7. Should graphic artists work with reporters to verify the information to be used on the graphic, or should art departments remain independent and separate from reporters?

8. What is a garbage graphic?

9. Describe a story that would be well-served by a data map.

Exercise V: Cutlines

Indicate whether each statement is true or false.

_____ 1. A cutline should only state things that are immediately apparent in the photo.

_____ 2. Always use phrases like "shown above" or "pictured here" in cutlines to help the reader.

_____ 3. When using an old file photo, the cutline or source line should explain the photo's age and origin.

_____ 4. The cutline should try to identify everyone visible in the photo.

Exercise VI: Problem Cutlines

Write brief answers to the following.

Situation #1: You are a copy editor. You are presented with a cutline for a photo illustrating a story about the collapse of a stretch of elevated freeway. In the foreground are two women obviously disturbed by the sight. In the background is the wreckage of the freeway and three automobiles, as well as assorted police and fire personnel. The cutline reads like this:

Joline Smith and Mary Jones react in shock and sadness at the sight of the Nimitz Freeway collapse yesterday.

Question: Is this a good cutline? If so, explain why. If not, explain how it could be improved. Write a different cutline, if needed.

Situation #2: You are presented with a cutline for a photo illustrating the crowd at the first game of the season for your local major league baseball team. In the foreground is a youngster wearing a logo jacket and holding up a banner. He's in the upper deck of the stadium. In the background is a panoramic view of the stadium, the field and other people in the crowd. The cutline reads like this:

This young fan came to Opening Day to fly the flag and root, root, root for the home team.

Question: Is this a good cutline? If so, explain why. If not, explain how it could be improved. Write a different cutline, if needed.

Situation #3: You are presented with a cutline for a photo of a Latino man behind the back window of a police vehicle. He is looking straight at the camera and appears to be very angry. The cutline reads like this:

Forgery suspect Jorge-Luis Ortega snarls at the camera after police arrest him at his Hayward home.

Question: Is this a good cutline? If so, explain why. If not, explain how it could be improved. Write a different cutline, if needed.

Situation #4: You are presented with a cutline for a photo of a Chinese man pulling a rickshaw on the streets of Beijing for a travel story. The cutline reads like this:

Travelers to Beijing can still see Chinamen pulling rickshaws on the city streets.

Question: Is this a good cutline? If so, explain why. If not, explain how it could be improved. Write a different cutline, if needed.

CHAPTER 12
Designing Pages

Exercise I: Story Selection for Front Page

You are the news editor. Rank the following stories for their potential use on Page 1 of your newspaper (1 = highest priority, 10 = lowest).

_____ **1.** A Supreme Court justice retires.

_____ **2.** A local woman wins $15 million in the state lottery.

_____ **3.** A local triple-murder case is thrown out of court on a technicality.

_____ **4.** The state treasurer gives a speech at a local school.

_____ **5.** A highway-finance bill affecting your community is rejected by a U.S. Senate sub-committee.

_____ **6.** A local teacher is cited by an actor during an Oscar-acceptance speech as being "a great influence in my life."

_____ **7.** The city council is scheduled to vote on the city budget tonight.

_____ **8.** A former beauty queen appears before the national press and claims that she had a longtime affair with a former president.

_____ **9.** A local chessmaster advances to the finals in an international chess competition in Finland.

_____ **10.** A local museum puts on display a previously unknown painting by Pablo Picasso.

Exercise II: Page Design Practice

Design a front page using your selections from the previous list, headlines, photos and fill-in text. Feel free to use promo boxes and whatever else you deem appropriate.

Exercise III: Page Design Vocabulary

Write brief descriptions for the following.

1. Contrast
2. Gray space
3. Teases
4. Gutters
5. Points of entry
6. Spot color
7. Superblurb
8. Modular layout
9. Points
10. Picas
11. Broadsheet
12. Tabloids

13. Bastard measures	27. Cutline
14. Glance boxes	28. Sans serif
15. Above the fold	29. Cutlines
16. Skewing	30. Jumpline
17. Wrapping	31. Byline
18. Raw wrap	32. Standing hed
19. Cropping	33. Initial cap
20. Agate	34. Display hed
21. Overprinting	35. Quoteout
22. Butting heads	36. Ear
23. Pagination	37. Folio line
24. Dominant visual	38. Standalone photo
25. The "dollar rule"	39. Skybox
26. Backward L wrap	

Exercise IV: Page Design Aesthetics

Indicate whether the following statements about page design are true or false.

_____ 1. The proportion wheel is an artifact of the pre-computer age and today's copy editors need not learn how to use it.

_____ 2. Newspaper design underwent a paradigm shift beginning in 1982, with the flashy design of USA Today.

_____ 3. The New York Times has never redesigned any of its sections, remaining steadfast in its classical layout traditions.

_____ 4. If you have a 12-inch story, you have a choice of three layout modules: two-column vertical, three-column horizontal or four-column horizontal.

_____ 5. How many inches tall is a 36-point headline?

_____ 6. How many inches wide is a 12-pica headline?

_____ 7. An interesting steeplechase wrap leads the reader's eye logically around the photograph.

_____ 8. Legs of type shorter than 2 inches generally keep the reader interested and actively engaged in a story.

Exercise V: Evaluating Front-Page Designs

Evaluate front-page layouts for your local daily and two national newspapers. Identify the elements used and evaluate how they all worked together. Offer suggestions for improvement. Tell what you liked and what you would have done differently.

Exercise VI: Re-Design

Pick a newspaper and re-design the look of its front page. Explain why you made the changes.